Low Cost Living

2nd Edition

John Harrison

....

A HOW TO BOOK

ROBINSON

ROBINSON

First published in Great Britain in 2018 by
Robinson

A CIP catalogue record for this book
is available from the British Library.

ISBN: 978-1-47213-718-0

Typeset in Sentinel by
Initial Typesetting Services, Edinburgh
Printed and bound in Great Britain by
Clays Ltd, St Ives plc

Papers used by Robinson are from well-
managed forests and other responsible
sources

MIX
Paper from
responsible sources
FSC® C104740

Robinson
An imprint of
Little, Brown Book Group
Carmelite House
50 Victoria Embankment
London EC4Y 0DZ

An Hachette UK Company
www.hachette.co.uk

www.littlebrown.co.uk

How To Books are published by
Robinson, an imprint of Little, Brown
Book Group. We welcome proposals
from authors who have first-hand
experience of their subjects.
Please set out the aims of your book,
its target market and its suggested
contents in an email to
Nikki.Read@howtobooks.co.uk

CONTENTS

Preface to the second edition

Since I wrote the first edition of this book some ten years ago, we've suffered the results of a banking collapse that nobody saw coming, despite it being so obvious (in hindsight) that lending people money that they could never pay back would lead to tears.

Rather than things getting better they've got worse for many – if not most of us – over the last decade.

Hopefully the tips and advice in this book will help you at least cope better with financial strains and pressure; or, better still, escape them.

At the same time we've seen climate change starting to hit home with so-called 'once-in-a-hundred-years' weather events like drought, storms and floods seemingly happening every year. Reducing carbon emissions and being greener are becoming more vital if disaster is to be avoided. Our practical ways of being green may not be the solution to the world's problems, but at least they help rather than add to them.

In this second edition I'm grateful for the opportunity to clarify and better explain some ideas that seem to have been misunderstood, and to correct some errors. It's also an opportunity to take account of changes and developments over the last decade.

Introduction

It's a paradox of modern life that we earn more money and enjoy a higher standard of living than ever before, yet we work longer hours and are reportedly more dissatisfied and unhappier than previous generations. It seems obvious that affluence doesn't lead to satisfaction. Indeed, as we have become more affluent we have also got more and more into debt. It truly seems that the more we have, the more we want.

I was quite surprised to discover in a recent report that my wife and I live just above the modern poverty line. I've never felt poor; I don't seem to need to spend much or want for much. I loathe waste and tend to think carefully about whatever I spend, but that doesn't mean I deny myself. I just don't feel the need to have the latest gadget the minute it arrives in the shops.

Much of our approach to life was learned from our parents and, even more so, our grandparents. In my grandmother's bathroom was a little plastic net into which she put the last bits of soap so that eventually she had a new bar and none was wasted. That's a prime example of 'waste not, want not'. My grandparents were not rich, but I never heard them complain about being poor. They were comfortable, warm and well fed from grandfather's garden and allotment.

Strangely this economical approach to life is not limited to the poor. In my working life, I've come across a number of rich people – I mean helicopter- and Bentley-owning rich. One thing I've noticed is that they don't waste either. They think through even small spending decisions. One chap showed me around his mansion (anything with twelve bedrooms is a mansion to me!) and, as we left each room, he switched out the lights. 'No point giving money to the electricity company,' was his comment.

That's not a bad attitude to have; after all, who needs the money most, you or the electricity company? It's an approach to cultivate. Being frugal and sensible doesn't mean you're mean or a skinflint; it's a way to enjoy a better life for less. Even the Queen is said to be frugal in her personal life, using Tupperware to keep her breakfast cereal fresh. Nice one, Your Majesty.

So, having seen the prices of many things fall while our incomes have increased over the years, why do we not all feel like contented millionaires? It's worth taking a little time to see where the money goes.

Much of our money nowadays is spent on keeping a roof over our heads. House prices may fall at times, but comparing property prices with average incomes shows a considerable rise in the last fifty years. In 1955 the average house cost £1,937 – just £44,000 at today's prices – but the average wage was the equivalent of £22,500 a year in today's money.

And don't forget that when the average wage was £22,500 only the man of the house was generally working. Now the average wage is near £27,600 and both partners are likely to be employed. Of course, you have to be careful with statistics, but it's fairly clear we pay a lot more for housing now than we did sixty-odd years ago.

There's not a lot you can do about rents or mortgages or council tax, apart from financial juggling (and I'll leave that to the experts who brought you the financial disaster of 2008). But it's not just housing that accounts for our money; what we put into those houses has a big part to play.

Fifty years ago a television was a real luxury. A huge box that sat in the corner of the parlour where the family would gather round to watch flickering black-and-white images. Now many households have more televisions than people living in the house.

There used to be just one telephone sat in the hallway. Now we have multiple cordless phones and everyone has a mobile, if not a smartphone as well. Even we have a mobile – it must need topping up soon as I put £10 on it just last year.

Before you spend out on something, ask yourself if you really want or need it. Will it make any difference to you if you don't buy it? You'll be amazed how many times the answer is that it won't improve your life one jot.

However, there are necessary expenses that you can easily take control of and reduce. You can reasonably reduce your energy bills without shivering in the dark. You can reduce your transport costs; you may need to change your lifestyle a bit, but you'll find it an improvement. It's about changing your approach to these things, and not about wearing a hair shirt and denying every pleasure in life.

Much of this book is about food; how to eat better-tasting and healthier food (and for far less than you might have thought). I make no apology for this. It is one area where you can really save money and improve the quality of your life at the same time.

I'm convinced that many of the illnesses we suffer are caused by the food we buy and eat. I don't mean things like food poisoning, as modern hygiene standards are superb. I mean the production methods all along the food chain increasing fats, sugar, salt and chemicals in our diet, along with a cocktail of pesticide residues. Proper, real food not only tastes good, it does you good and generally costs you less money (although you may pay more for organic, pesticide-free food).

In the 1970s, we and many others were inspired by books such as John Seymour's *Complete Book of Self Sufficiency* and TV programmes like *The Good Life*. Of course, these were more inspirational than practical. Even in the 1970s a suburban garden in London was unlikely to be large enough to be an urban farm, although I do recall Tom and Barbara got an allotment in one episode. Mr Seymour's wonderful book did rather presuppose you had five acres in the country and no need to earn money to pay a mortgage while you did everything for yourself.

It was inspiring for all that, though. Although we didn't have that smallholding, we did find there were a lot of things we could do for ourselves in an ordinary house and garden.

No, we don't grow our own wheat and grind our own flour, but we do bake our own bread. We don't have a pig or a small house cow on the patio, but we can have fresh eggs and free-range chicken, and honey from a beehive.

Above all, the suggestions in this book are practical. Everything I recommend is either something we or our friends do or have done. Things that make sense financially and which make a reasonable trade-off between your time and money. They make sense ecologically as well. Low-cost living is also most often environmentally low-impact living.

There's no point in spending hours and hours doing something you hate just to save a few pennies. However, if you enjoy doing something it isn't work. So if you save money while having fun, then that's great by my reckoning.

To give you a couple of examples: I love growing my own vegetables. It's interesting, satisfying and good exercise. If you hate it and find it nothing but a chore, then don't do it. Use your time on another money-saving or money-making hobby instead.

In this book I explain how we make our own butter. One method we came across involved either putting cream into a jar and shaking it for hours, or buying special churning jars with paddles. You can forget that nonsense. If you've ever over-whipped cream, then you know it turns into butter. Guess how we do it? I like butter, but I'm not daft enough to spend hours shaking a jar.

Like most people nowadays we're trying to be green, or at least greener. We don't want to pass an ecological disaster on to our children or grandchildren, after all. I firmly believe climate change is a real danger and if we don't take action now it could be too late to avert a disaster that we can only imagine. Perhaps not for a hundred years, but I don't want to be cursed by future generations.

However, it is pointless making theoretical suggestions that only the biggest eco-fanatic is likely to carry out, or suggesting things that cost a fortune so only the wealthy can afford to do them.

There's an awful lot of money being made out of people's desire to be green. What makes me angry are those gadgets that salve a guilty conscience but do no more than that. One good example of this is someone I know who has bought a timer for his shower so that he cuts down his water use. No matter that he has a power shower that delivers enough water to fill the average bath in 10 minutes, when an ordinary shower would just pop an inch of water into the bath over the same time. Forget his poorly insulated loft – he's 'green' because he has a shower timer.

Real solutions that reduce our impact on the environment may not be sexy – they may even be positively boring – but they work, and people can and will use them.

So I hope this book will help you to enjoy a better quality of life by spending less money and also help the planet because you are living a greener lifestyle. You'll find there is more on this subject on my website: www.lowcostliving.co.uk.

CHAPTER ONE

Low-cost eating

If you look at the real cost of food as a proportion of the household budget over the years, it has fallen. Our rents and mortgages zoom up, and the price of fuel goes up, but the food we eat is cheaper now than ever before.

We're generally wealthier now, but because these other costs – especially housing costs – have risen so much we have less money available to spend on food. The food budget is one thing we're very aware of and can control, which really increases the pressure on suppliers to meet our demands for cheap food.

This reduction in food cost has been achieved in part by our farming industry becoming far more productive. Mechanisation, a huge armoury of chemicals, and cheap labour imported from poorer countries have enabled the farmer to supply food to the industry at a lower price than at any other time in our history.

Cheap food comes at a cost

This increase in cost efficiency from the farming industry has not been without consequences. There has been damage to the environment from increased chemical use and large-scale farming. Run-off from slurry into fields and subsequently pollution of rivers, destruction of habitat resulting in a reduction in the number of wild birds, and the use of a number of pesticides are all implicated in the catastrophic decline in bees, which are vital to pollination of most crops, as well as flowers.

The pressure on the farmer to supply cheaper food has resulted in the horror of chickens kept so crowded that the poor things can hardly move. Modern meat chickens have been bred so that they reach selling weight quicker, but at the cost of growing faster than their legs can support. And that's just one example of the decline in animal welfare that the pressure for ever-cheaper food has brought about. Finally, the ethics of importing cheap labour from less fortunate countries to work at jobs British workers don't want, at wages British workers would not accept, is debatable at best.

Farmers are only one link in the chain, though. Next come the food manufacturers. They're under the same financial pressure to supply cheap food and so they look to cut costs and add value wherever they can.

I'll touch on the Chorleywood process in Chapter 8 – the introduction of 'industrial' bread-making techniques in the early 1960s – but it applies to nearly all the food we buy. It's quite ironic that one of the reasons for the formation of the co-operative movement back in 1843 was to provide wholesome food. The producers and retailers at the time were also reacting to financial pressures and were adulterating foods to reduce costs.

Nowadays we have masses of legislation to protect us, but it still gives the manufacturer a lot of room to manoeuvre and reduce costs. Nearly 170 years later we no longer get floor sweepings in our food, but we do get mechanically reclaimed meat. Let's look at some examples.

Chicken

To start with something simple that you wouldn't think could be messed about with, let's look at chickens. The cheap, 'densely raised' chicken has more fat content than the free-range one, but the manufacturers don't stop there. By splitting the chicken into components, they increase its monetary value. This is why you can buy breasts, legs, wings, etc, separately. It may be more convenient than jointing your own, but you pay for the privilege.

The next step is to increase the selling price further by adding water, thus increasing weight. It is perfectly legal for the processors to add as much water as they want, i.e. as much as they think they can get away with, to your chicken. Often it's just 15 per cent of the weight, but it has been known to be as high as 40 per cent. So you end up paying for water.

If they just injected water it would drain away, so they use polyphosphates to bind the water into the chicken. Polyphosphates are approved for use as an additive in food and considered safe, although a preliminary study published in the *American Journal of Respiratory and Critical Care Medicine* in 2007 suggests they may be implicated in lung cancer. Average consumption of these chemicals has about doubled over the last ten years.

While they're at it, they add some salt and dextrose (a sugar) to the water, to 'improve' the flavour and disguise the 'wateryness' of the product. Never mind that too much salt and sugar are bad for health; this is perfectly legal.

So we move from a healthy lean meat to a product that is high in fat, salt and sugar and might even increase your risk of lung cancer. If you buy some cheap chicken, check the label; you could have an unpleasant surprise.

Processed meat products

It's not just chicken that gets the bulking treatment. Have you ever wondered why cheap bacon shrinks so much? The water boils off when you cook it. It's perfectly legal but you have to wonder how much would sell if it had '15 per cent water' in bold letters on the front of the pack rather than '85 per cent pork' in the ingredients list that you need good eyesight to read.

When we move onto more processed foods and food products, the situation gets worse. A meat pie may only be 18 per cent meat. Some of the remaining 82 per cent is the pastry, but the actual meat is bulked up with various things including connective tissues (the stringy bits the butcher throws away) and even chicken skin.

The other wonder they give us is mechanically reclaimed meat. This consists of the bits that adhere to the bones, skin and so forth that would be thrown away by any self-respecting cook at home. It comes out as an unappetising paste, but that's no problem to the food scientists who can easily add some chemicals, salt and sugar to make it taste like food when it goes into a product. Sausages are an obvious target for these meat-like products. The budget sausage may have as little as 40 per cent meat and that includes the mechanically reclaimed connective tissues and chicken skins.

It's quite common and traditional to add breadcrumbs to breakfast sausage. They're not just a bulking agent but improve the texture and succulence. Rusk, however, does the same job but is nutritionally poorer than breadcrumbs. Guess what goes into the cheap mass-produced sausage?

Low-cost eating isn't the same as eating cheap food

The reason I have touched on what much of the food we buy actually consists of is to emphasise that low-cost eating is not the same as buying cheap food. I'm neither a food snob nor a gourmet, but there is no way I would touch a pack of sausages that cost 2p each to buy. I am convinced that 99 per cent of us wouldn't eat cheap foods if we'd seen how they're made. My one week of temp work as a lad in the pie factory was enough to put me off those pies for life.

With a little thought and planning, you can reduce the cost of your food considerably *and* be assured of what you are eating. There's a lot of medical evidence that we eat far too much meat – and especially red meat – for our own good. We're genetically programmed to like the taste of meat and fats – they're high in energy and protein. Now we can all get as much as we want. No longer do we make do with some grains because the mammoth escaped the hunting party. The result is bowel cancer, heart disease and obesity.

Meat is certainly the most expensive part of our diet, both financially and ecologically, so eating less is a good idea. However, it's easier said than done to say 'eat less meat' as the vast majority of us like it. Even some vegetarians will admit they liked the taste of meat; I suspect many others just don't admit it. My way of reducing the amount of meat we eat, as well as the cost, is effective and, most importantly, enables us to eat meat that tastes just as good. In fact, I would say better.

For a start, let's consider cheap cuts of meat. Brisket and braising steak have wonderful flavour but cost far less than rump steak. Neck of lamb is as cheap as chips and costs a pittance in comparison with a leg, but the flavour is, in my opinion, better.

Now there is a problem with these cheaper cuts in that they need to be cooked slowly and properly. We find that marinating and slowly cooking them results in a melt-in-your-mouth texture as well as a superior flavour to more expensive cuts. Marinating in wine doesn't just add flavour; the acid tenderises the meat. So do give cheaper cuts a try.

Don't forget offal. I find it strange that people who happily eat a cow's bottom (that's a rump steak) recoil in horror at kidneys and liver. Interestingly, the Inuit people (living in the Arctic regions of the world) who eat little apart from meat consider these parts to be the best. That's probably due to them having more vitamins and iron. If you've not tried them, why not give it a go? At worst you won't like the taste.

That's reduced the cost, so let's look at the quantity next. Slow cooking will create a superb gravy, delighting our taste buds with that 'umami' meat flavour, but we still like that meat texture. Just like the food factory we add a bulking agent, but our bulking agents are good for you. Mushrooms are brilliant for this. The ordinary cheap mushrooms are a little bland but they'll absorb the meat flavour and add that texture we crave. We also use beans a lot with meat dishes. Beans are as rich in protein as most meat, have the same sort of texture and are just as filling.

We grow our own vegetables and I always end up with too many runner beans so I let them grow on and the actual beans develop. These are ideal for adding to stews and casseroles. We use a lot of home-grown broad beans too, but if you don't grow your own, red kidney beans work well.

Don't buy beans in tins; instead buy dried beans, which are far cheaper. Most just need soaking overnight to rehydrate them and they are ready to add to a slow-cooking dish. If you're pushed for time, having forgotten to soak some beans the night before, you can get away with a fast-soaking method. Rinse the beans in a colander or sieve, then put into a large saucepan and cover with water to about three or four times the volume of beans. Bring them to a fast boil and keep boiling for 4 or 5 minutes. Switch off the heat and leave covered for an hour.

Note: it is important to boil red kidney beans vigorously for 10 minutes after soaking, and then change the water. Boil again and discard the water. These beans contain a high level of haemagglutinins, which can cause a serious gastric upset. This process reduces the level to that found in all beans.

If you have freezer room, you can pre-cook beans and freeze them for use later. We do this with chickpeas which are so versatile, not just for hummus and falafel, but for bean burgers (see page 16) and bean salads. We also freeze portions of red kidney beans, which go well to stretch any meat casserole as well as chilli con carne.

You can make a very acceptable chilli without the meat, too, as red kidney beans are so satisfying.

For bulk cooking beans, you can't beat a pressure cooker. Chickpeas take between an hour and an hour and a half to cook in a saucepan, but just 20–30 minutes in a pressure cooker. Pre-soaked beans also work well in slow-cooker meals.

While we're on the subject of dried beans, please don't buy those tubs of hummus. It is so easy to make (see opposite), and dried chickpeas are very inexpensive.

Beans and pulses have a health benefit as well as being a money saver. As I've said, they're high in protein, but – unlike meats – there's no fat and they're high in fibre. Great for your cholesterol levels and bowel health. Lack of fibre and red meats are implicated in bowel cancer.

There's a lot to be said for a vegetarian or vegan diet both for our individual health and the ecology, but some land is only really suitable for pasturing animals. I think we'd all be a lot better off if us omnivores stopped eating meat as a standard and moved to a low-meat diet.

Apart from meat, people spend a fortune on ready-prepared foods. From pasties to pies, we keep those factories running. Unfortunately, you may well find it actually costs you more to make your own than to buy a cheap one ready made, and wonder why you should bother.

The reason is that making your own means you know what has gone into your meal – and I promise you it will be better than nearly anything you buy. Would you put chicken skin into your steak pie? If you make an apple tart will you add stabilisers and bulking agents?

Some low-cost recipes

Here are just a couple of our favourite recipes. The ingredients are cheap, but the results taste anything but. As with all our recipes, we adapt to what we have available so don't be afraid to change things.

Hummus

The price of this in the shops never fails to amaze me; it is so cheap to make and it tastes more wicked than it is. I tend to soak and cook a batch of dried chickpeas and freeze them so that they're on hand when the urge takes me. Technically you should use tahini in this, which is sesame cream, but I don't like the taste. You probably could make this by crushing the chickpeas and sieving them, but it is far easier with a food processor.

Method

- Put a good handful of chickpeas into the processor along with a crushed clove of garlic and add olive oil and lemon juice in a ratio of two tablespoons of oil to one of lemon juice. Whizz until it becomes creamy. If it is a little dry, add more oil and lemon juice or a little water until the consistency is correct.
- Taste and add a little salt if you think it needs it.
- Put it into a ramekin-style serving dish, cover with cling film and chill in the fridge until needed.

Bean burgers

Bean burgers are low fat, have plenty of healthy dietary fibre and are very cheap to make. But don't let that put you off – they taste fantastic! The beauty of them is that you can make them with different types of bean, add herbs or not, make them spicy or plain, whatever you like. I'm sure you would never need to repeat. You can also add nuts, but I don't think that works too well.

Ingredients

Makes four good-sized burgers.

1/2 onion, diced

2 or more cloves of garlic, crushed or chopped very finely

500g (1lb 2oz) cooked mixed beans

herbs and/or spices to suit (a chopped dried chilli pepper certainly adds zing)

1 medium carrot, grated or chopped finely

50g (2oz) breadcrumbs (fresh work best)

1 egg, beaten

Method

- Fry the onion and garlic in a little oil until soft and then whizz everything into a food processor. Could not be easier!
- Divide into four portions and form into burgers before frying or grilling on a medium heat.
- Serve just as you would meat burgers.

CHAPTER TWO

Beating the super-markets at their own game

Love them or hate them, the fact is that the vast majority of us shop in supermarkets. The corner grocery shop has become a very rare beast.

The supermarkets' success is based on offering us what we want, when we want it, at a competitive price. That's why we shop there. Being huge, they can stock nearly everything you may want. Many are now open every hour the law allows and also available online, which has killed the last advantage of the 'open all hours' corner shop.

Supermarkets may be open when you want, but are they really competitive?

Some years back I was told by an insider in the supermarket business that it wasn't how cheap you were that mattered but how cheap your customers *thought* you were that mattered. In other words, if they could fool you they would.

As a business, they are incredibly sophisticated at parting you from your cash. Just the position of goods in the store – and even on the shelf within a section – makes a difference to how much they sell. That's why they have entire dummy stores in which to test ideas and find the most efficient way to empty your wallet.

Then there are the offers. Buy One, Get One Free! Half Price! Price Crunch! Rollback! The list goes on and on. Unsurprisingly most people find this bewildering – and if you think about it, a bewildered customer is not too bad a thing from the supermarkets' viewpoint.

I don't want to suggest that any of this is wrong; the supermarkets scrupulously obey the laws of the land. But make no mistake, the duty (in law!) of the management is to make the maximum profit for the benefit of the shareholders. They are not a charity, and they do not have your best interests at heart. It's *their* best interests that matters to them.

That's not to say they're all the same. Some do take social responsibility seriously, while others just give it lip service. The Co-op and Waitrose are particularly good, which I would think is down to their different ownership structures. The Co-op is owned by its members (anyone can join) and the profits are shared amongst them. Waitrose is owned by the John Lewis Partnership which shares out the organisation's profits amongst the staff who are known as partners.

Now that we know the underlying truths in our relationship with most of the supermarkets, let's play the game to win.

Decide what you need

This may seem pretty obvious – you may think most people are capable of shopping according to need – until you see the figures on wasted food. Surveys show that up to a third of the food we buy is thrown away. Examples are quoted of people buying the same items each week, returning home and throwing away the same item they'd bought the week before.

I found this unbelievable, but then I saw someone do just that. She was packing the shopping away, took a packet of Brie cheese from the fridge, unopened, and dropped it in the bin. Then she put the new packet into the fridge. Yes, I fished out the old packet and it was still within its 'use by' date.

It's so simple: keep a pencil and pad of paper in the kitchen and note anything that you are running out of. This is called a shopping list! If it is not on the list, then you don't need it.

Be aware of prices

When I was a youth I worked in my father's supermarket. It may have been tiny by modern standards but the principles were the same. He offered good prices to get sales, but to get these prices and still make a profit he had to buy at the best price. This meant that he knew how much things were and he could spot a bargain at twenty paces.

You need to be aware of what things costs. Don't just drop things into the trolley – look at the price. Pretty soon you will find you have a good idea of what you should be paying and will pick up on price increases or the same product being cheaper down the road at another supermarket.

Don't assume that the packets are the same size, either. We noticed that Arborio rice had dropped in price but on closer inspection the packet size had decreased, from 1,000g to 750g. The actual cost per 100g had gone up by 20 per cent.

Some supermarket shelves carry labels detailing the price per 100g of the product on display, or such like, but it's no big deal to take a small calculator with you and check for yourself. It also helps you remember the price for next time.

Don't assume the larger packet is better value, either. I've lost count of the number of times it has actually been cheaper to buy smaller packets than large. This seems to apply frequently to tea bags.

Often you'll find a massive stack of a product at the end of an aisle and think it's on offer or must be a good price. Not always. We've found that sometimes a similar product on the shelf is better value in a different pack size.

I'm not saying it's deliberate, but the best value-for-money items are often on the bottom shelves. The shelves at your eye level are going to move goods fastest, so logically the most profitable ones for the shop are going to be there. Remember those test stores where they plan the layouts? There's good reason for that investment.

As you pay for your shopping don't just pack away. Check the price as it goes through the till and, before you walk out of the store, scan down the receipt. I think we end up going back to customer services with a mistake about one in five shopping trips. Strangely, we can't think of a time when we have found a mistake in our favour.

Sometimes they take an offer off the computer and forget to take the price off the shelf; other times they put an offer on the shelf and haven't got around to changing the computer price.

Reduced goods are high risk for mistakes. They get scanned at full price or have been further reduced and the wrong price is scanned. It may only be a few pence, but they are your pennies. Give them to charity by all means – but our supermarkets aren't a charity.

Working the offers

Take no notice of how offers are promoted. All that actually matters is the price you pay. Whether this is half price or even a quarter of some previous price doesn't matter a jot. That's not to say you should ignore the advertising; just don't presume something really is a good deal because they tell you it is.

You should make the offers work for you. We've noticed that the supermarkets have patterns to their offers. It varies between the different outlets, but basically something comes on offer for a period, is off for a period and then back on again.

Many of the things we buy regularly will store for a long time. Checking our cupboard, the tinned goods seem to have about a year's shelf life. We bulk buy many staples on offer, then restock the next time they're on offer.

What isn't on offer in one shop may well be on offer in another. If you don't have time to go to more than one supermarket a week, vary which one you use. This will expose you to different offers and help train you in how much things cost. We're fortunate in having five supermarkets near to each other and tend to visit three in a trip. It takes a little more time but pays us back in the overall bill.

After a while you begin to get a feel for offers. Perhaps you're down to a couple of tins of beans or the last carton of tea bags, but you know they'll be coming on offer next week so you hold on. We even know the days the offers change in the store now, but amazingly it seems to vary between areas even in the same chain.

Loyalty cards and vouchers

I suppose if there was anything like a perfect customer for a supermarket, it's someone who is time-poor who runs in, buys what he/she wants regardless of price and drives into the distance until next week.

Since such people are in short supply, some of the chains go to great lengths to turn you into a loyal little consumer. In the old days, they used to give Green Shield stamps with your purchase, which you would stick into books and then trade the books for cash. The idea was that you would go to the shop offering them rather than the one that didn't.

The modern equivalent is the loyalty card, but now it's far more sophisticated. Of course part of the idea is that the more you use it, the more money or points to exchange for discounts build up.

The real benefit to the store is that they know what you buy. They develop a profile of you and can tailor their adverts. There is little point in offering you cheap dog food if you keep a cat.

It's a little scary how much they know about you, but that's the way of the world. I suppose it's just an enormous, computerised version of the time when the shopkeeper knew his customers and their favourite brands.

It's well worth going through all the vouchers they send you and using them, so long as you were going to buy that product anyway. Don't forget the basic rule of checking the price: 20p off something that is 30p dearer than elsewhere is no bargain at all.

They also like to send you vouchers for £2 off when you spend £20. We make use of these by buying what we normally would plus something that we can store and is on sale at a good price. If you just spend £20 the discount is 10 per cent but they hope that you will go in and spend £30, making it just 6.66 per cent. We feel we've lost if the shopping comes to more than £21 on a £20 voucher buy.

Don't forget, there's usually nothing to stop you using two vouchers at the same time. So you get your 20p off cheese and your £2 off the overall purchase. After all, they're encouraging you to buy with these offers, so it would be silly not to use them.

Manager's reductions

This is where you can really win with your shopping so long as you're prepared to use your freezer. Many products will have a little symbol and the magic words 'Suitable for Home Freezing'.

When you see this you know you can safely buy something with a short date life, freeze it and use it later when you want it.

All the foodstuffs you buy will have a date on them. Usually the format is 'Display Until' and a date, followed by 'Use By' and a date. Once those dates are passed the shop cannot sell the item to you, even if it is perfectly good and safe. If by chance there was something wrong and you got food poisoning, they would be in awful trouble.

As the date on these items approaches, the goods are reduced to clear, and if they have not sold reduced further. Once the day is past, it is game over and the food is dumped.

If you shop a lot, you will get to know when they do this checking and price reduction. Different stores tend to have different times. Sadly for the bargain hunter, more and more people are catching on to these short-life offers, which means there is competition for them.

Once we came across a supermarket closing for redevelopment and half filled a large chest freezer with enough butter to last us a year at a quarter of its normal price. We enjoyed a Chateaubriand reduced from £25 to £5, and the finest organic chicken at less than half price (with one for the cats to share as well). It's fantastic what you can find if you keep your eyes open and you're in the right place at the right time.

One thing to watch out for is reduced items where they are on a 'Buy One Get One Free' or 'Two For £5' type of offer. Some stores will apply the discount at the till, and others won't.

We managed one year to go through the checkout after Christmas with two trolleys full of bargains like Stilton cheeses, smoked salmon and so on. The poor bewildered operator called the manager, who said they owed us £3.56 and would we mind buying something else as they couldn't refund!

How it works is that something costing £1.50 on 'Buy One Get One Free' is calculated by the computer as £1.50, add £1.50 and then take off £1.50. Since the item had been reduced to 50p it happily charged us for two 50p purchases and then deducted £1.50. Yes, they can pay you to take luxury food away.

Unfortunately most supermarkets have caught onto this now. If you buy something with a cover price of, say, £3 reduced to £2 but it's on an offer of 'Buy Two for £5' your real saving is not £1 but just 50p. It takes a little thinking about, but it pays to be attentive.

Many supermarkets have counter service for meat, fish and delicatessen products. Towards the end of the day you can pick up some bargains as they prepare to close down for the night. We've actually haggled here. When we asked how much if we cleared the lot, we got a load of meat reduced to half the already reduced price. On a subsequent visit, the chap recognised us and asked if we would be interested in the pork chops as he could reduce them if we took them all.

Haggling is an art most of us have forgotten nowadays, unless we holiday in Morocco or somewhere similar. The trick is not to take the first offer, never appear too keen or bothered and be prepared to walk away, even if you have to appear to have second thoughts and go back with a final offer.

Other shopping tips

Try to avoid shopping on busy days and at busy times. On a quiet Tuesday you have time and space to look at the options, and towards the end of the day there will be drastic manager's reductions to be had. On a busy Friday or Saturday you'll be lucky to find a bargain and you'll be too busy fighting the crowd to think properly.

Never go food shopping when you are hungry. It's purely psychological, but you'll find you spend far more when you are hungry. You'll buy things you wouldn't normally because you fancy eating them, and you'll rush because you're in a hurry to get home and eat.

Try the value or own label products. Sometimes they're rubbish compared with the branded products, but sometimes it is exactly the same product in the tin with a different label. I once saw a packet of biscuits from a well-known manufacturer with three labels. The main wrapper was for the branded product and the label at each end was for two different supermarkets' own label versions.

Food safety

When buying reduced short-life foods you need to understand the dating system and how to store your bargain safely. Salmonella is no joke.

The first date you may see is 'Display Until' or 'Sell By'. These are not required by law but are more of an instruction to the shop's staff. The dates you actually need to concern yourself with are 'Use By' and 'Best Before'.

'**Use By**' is found on things with a short shelf life, like cooked meats or fish or pork pies. It's important that you store chilled foods as instructed. If something is safe in a fridge for two days, it may only be safe on the worktop for 6 hours. 'Use By' does not mean 'Eat By', though. You can freeze your bargain and keep it until you are ready, assuming it is suitable, but when you defrost it the clock has restarted. Don't store it for too long in the freezer, either. See the instructions on freezing food in Chapter 6.

Don't risk it with 'Use By' dates. The item may look and smell fine but would be breeding bacteria and have become dangerous.

Even if meats and fish have gone past their 'Use By' date and are unsafe for us, we find our pet cat will appreciate them. Their guts are different from ours and they can eat things that will make us ill. For legal reasons, that's not a suggestion that you do the same or treat that as advice.

'Best Before' is more forgiving. It merely indicates that the food is now past its best and is perhaps starting to lose flavour. The date on a tin is 'Best Before', as on dried or frozen foods. Some 'Best Before' dates really don't make any difference and I'm sure they're only there because they're legally required. Use your own judgement.

There is one exception to this: eggs. Once past their date, they could contain salmonella and become potentially harmful. You could freeze them, as covered in Chapter 13.

Is the supermarket the best buy?

The supermarkets have spent a lot of money convincing us that they offer the best choice, quality and price, but do they? There's little doubt that for a product like a tin of beans you won't beat their price. One of the reasons those thousands of corner shops have died away is that they can't buy cheaper from the wholesaler than the supermarket sells for at retail on many products.

There are some independent retailers who can compete, though. Markets are sadly in decline but they can offer fantastic value as well as superb quality. We've noticed free-range eggs from a market stall at a third less than the best price in the supermarket. And a picture of the farm and hens that laid them, proudly displayed behind the counter!

Quality meat and fish can be found in markets as well. I'm talking about normal markets open just a couple of days a week, by the way. The special farmers' markets in our experience tend to offer over priced products, trading on the fact they're direct from the farm. We've seen a stall on a farmers' market offering Bury black puddings at twice the price of exactly the same black puddings in the indoor market.

Not everything is a bad deal at farmers' markets, but do be careful not to get carried away thinking you are buying something special when you're not.

A local butcher (whether on a market or in a shop) is hard-pressed to compete with the buying power of our major chains. However, if you're willing to bulk buy, then you can often end up with better quality for lower prices than the supermarkets. Just ask; they want to sell their meat to you and they're not stupid. They know it's a tough market and who their competitors are. If you buy half a pig or lamb including the less popular cuts, it's a 'win-win' situation: they'll be happy and you'll have a bargain for your freezer.

Regardless of the price, it's much nicer to enjoy high-quality meats, preferably locally reared in humane conditions, than to eat low quality. If you can get it for the same price, then why not?

In recent years chicken has become a staple low-cost product. Despite people protesting that they want quality of life for chickens, when it comes to actually spending money their moral scruples seem to be forgotten. If you can find a local supplier of free-range poultry, you can certainly buy whole chickens for less than the supermarket sells similar products for, although you won't beat the price for the battery hen.

If a better life for your food isn't important to you, be aware that studies have shown that free-range chickens contain less of the harmful fats in comparison with cruelly raised chickens. In other words, they're better for your health.

Farm shops can be a good source of value vegetables if you don't grow your own. Items like potatoes by the sack can be a lot cheaper than those washed potatoes in little plastic bags. Box schemes can be remarkably good value as well. Because they put together a selection of seasonal vegetables and so on the contents vary, but this is a good thing. It forces you to think a bit about what you're eating, and variations in diet are good for us.

If you live in or near a city with an Asian population, grab the opportunity to buy rice and pulses such as lentils at a low price from Asian stores. Often they'll sell rice in sacks and the price will be far lower than the small packets in the supermarket. Kept dry, rice will store well for a long time. My experience has been that these shopkeepers are really helpful and friendly as well, so don't be afraid to ask if you don't see what you want or don't know what you're looking at.

CHAPTER THREE

Cooking your food

How you cook your food can make a difference to your bills – and to your time. In World War II, when fuel saving was a patriotic duty, the government encouraged the use of pressure cooking, haybox cooking and multi-level saucepans. All just as valid today – but don't ignore the latest cooking methods, such as the halogen oven.

Microwaves

It's quite fashionable amongst foodies to dismiss microwave ovens. The truth is that they are very efficient for heating up or cooking small quantities and invaluable for rapidly defrosting food. They run at around 65–75 per cent efficiency, which is very high. In other words, for every 100 watts used, 70 watts is actually delivered into the food.

Conventional ovens use much of their energy input in bringing the air in the oven cavity up to temperature. In a microwave the energy just bounces around the cavity until it hits a water molecule in the food. That's why the cooking time is so short.

Of course, they don't brown food (unless you have a built-in grill), and when you get into larger quantities they take longer, so there is a point where you are better off with your conventional oven.

We had a wonderful machine with optimum programs for cooking various foods (or you could program it yourself). It came with a built-in browning grill and various accessories and cost quite a lot of money.

After three years the display went so it was uncontrollable and unrepairable. We thought about it and realised we'd never used any of the programs (I think you needed a degree in computer science to work them out anyway). Neither had we used the browning grill nor any of the accessories. It also had a clock that was always on using power, so it cost £8 a year to run before we actually used it.

The replacement cost us a tenth of the first model and merely has a mechanical timer and power settings. It looked as good, cooked as well and it lasted eight years.

Halogen ovens

Halogen hobs have been around for a long time, but using the same technology for an oven is relatively new. They cook quickly, typically twice as fast as a conventional oven. A roast chicken, properly browned along with roast potatoes and vegetables, takes just 35 minutes in a 1,400w machine.

They're not expensive to buy; an adequate halogen oven can be had for £30 to £40. The drawback is their small capacity, but many of us tend to underfill our normal ovens anyway. Unless you're cooking for a large family it's less of a problem than you may imagine.

Conventional cookers

There are few more personal choices than cookers. We swear by gas, some by electricity, and others by the Aga. Of course, you have to be rich to own an Aga. They look wonderful and impress visitors but they cost a small fortune and are not exactly cheap to run.

A few things to note if you're buying a new cooker. The actual oven size can vary greatly. I know of 600mm-wide cookers that have the same oven size as a 500mm version. It's worth taking a tape measure and checking when you buy a new cooker. A large oven costs practically the same to run as a small one, but it's so useful to have the extra space at Christmas and when batch cooking.

There's not much to choose in running costs between gas and electric cookers so it really comes down to personal preference. Even when we've not had mains gas, we've used LPG which was a little more expensive. With electric ovens our experience is that those with fan systems cook better and more efficiently than conventional ovens as the moving air ensures that hot air is always next to the food, so they save a little money as well.

Whatever your cooker, it makes sense to use the oven full. It takes no more energy to cook a full oven than a near-empty one. Always try to use an oven efficiently. If you're roasting a joint, then why not roast potatoes or vegetables at the same time? Or you could cook a pie or rice pudding together.

We tend to do a lot of batch cooking. It's not a lot more effort to make four lasagnes than one, or half a dozen loaves of bread. One for now and the rest go into the freezer. This efficient use of our time means we can still cook and eat properly even when we're busy, and it also cuts our energy usage.

Pressure cookers

Our pressure cooker is thirty-five years old and still works like new. We've replaced seals and valves along the way, of course, but we certainly get our money's worth from it. The theory of pressure cooking is quite simple. Water boils at 100°C (212°F) at sea level but the boiling point rises as pressure increases and lowers as it decreases, which is why mountaineers can't get a decent cup of tea. The water boils at too low a temperature.

Pressure cookers increase the boiling point so you cook the food at a higher temperature, saving energy as well as time. They're a bit of a fiddle and we wouldn't bother if we were just cooking a few potatoes for the two of us, but for bulk cooking they're well worth it.

When we harvest our carrots, often there are damaged ones that won't store well. As we love mashed carrots, we'll make a batch and freeze them. Then it's just a matter of taking a pack out of the freezer to go with Sunday lunch.

Mashed carrot is very easy to make. Just clean and cut the carrots into chunks and then cook for 5 minutes on high pressure. Reduce to room temperature and mash with a potato masher, adding salt and pepper to taste, and butter. I find white pepper works best, by the way. Another variation is half and half with parsnips or swedes. All these root vegetables take ages to boil normally in bulk but just 5 minutes in the pressure cooker. Because of the sweetness of the carrots they go down well with children, but hold back on the pepper. You can always add it to your serving.

Pressure cookers are great for making a stock as well. Usually this takes a few hours on the hob but you can reduce this to 40 minutes in a pressure cooker. You can cook entire meals with a pressure cooker, but we tend just to use ours where there is a clear benefit in saving time and energy. It's a bit like those books on microwave cooking that tell you how to cook everything in there. For some things they're excellent but, for others, it's a triumph of recipe writing over common sense.

Hob cooking

When cooking on the hob, a good tip is to always use a lid on your saucepan. You'll find that liquids reach boiling point about a third faster with a lid on, and you can maintain a fast boil even with the ring turned down to minimum. I don't know quite how much it saves in energy, but it has to mount up and costs nothing. It stops the kitchen getting full of steam as well, which brings us nicely round to steamers.

If you're boiling one vegetable, then why not steam another at the same time? The steamer tops that fit on a saucepan enable you literally to get double or even triple value from the one hob ring.

The kettle

Most modern electric kettles are capable of boiling just one cup of water but we insist on half filling them. Using our little power meter, I discovered we were wasting about £10 a year just on this. Now if £10 is nothing to you, my address to send it to is at the end of this book! Seriously, with 23 million households in the UK, that's £230 million pounds worth of electricity a year just from overfilling kettles. Being kind to your pocket is often the same as being kind to the planet.

Slow cooking – build a modern haybox cooker

Some years ago we bought a slow cooker. It was quite neat, being basically a large casserole dish with an electric cable, and only drawing 100 watts so not greedy either. The idea was that we could assemble a dish in the slow cooker in the morning, switch it on and return home from work to a hot meal. Slow cooking is excellent for those cheap cuts of meat we like so we thought it made perfect sense. Unfortunately, it didn't quite work like that. The food was burnt and stuck on the base and had acquired that horrible burnt food taste. Not exactly appetising. We realised it was just taking too long with us being out of the house for 9 hours.

Having said that, slow cookers have improved over the years. Now they have high and low settings, timers and can even hold at a serving temperature after cooking for a preset time until you return home. They're not expensive, either. We've seen them from as little as £12, but the better ones run from around £25.

Anyway, I read about an old method of cooking in a haybox and we decided to give that a try. The haybox is quite simply a box – any old cardboard box will do – lined with hay. We used the bedding bought for the rabbit hutch. The theory is you bring the casserole to the boil on the hob, cover it then put the dish into the box, stuffing some hay around and over it.

To our surprise this worked in that the food cooked without burning, but the problem now was it was going a bit cold when we got home.

So I decided to build a modern version of the haybox. We'd been doing some building work and had some surplus polystyrene insulation sheets used in the cavity walls, so there was the answer. I lined the box with the sheets, which provided much better insulation than the rabbit's hay. When we put the circular casserole dish into the square box, we filled the gaps with some polystyrene packing chips and that was that.

The food was perfectly cooked – no burnt taste – and piping hot when we got home. You can often get polystyrene packaging from electrical stores for free and the packing chips when you have something delivered. A cooker for free has to be good.

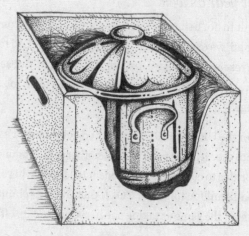

Fig. 1. A haybox.

CHAPTER FOUR

Food waste

In 2008, a study by the Waste & Resources Action Programme revealed that we throw away about a third of the food we buy. Worse still, 61 per cent of that food is perfectly edible. They worked out that the average family with children was spending £610 a year on food they didn't even eat – and this was before the dramatic increase in food prices later that year as well.

I must admit to not believing this when it was reported on the news; after all, we couldn't be that stupid, could we? Sad to say, it was well researched and we *are* being that stupid. Subsequent studies have shown a small improvement, down to 20 to 25 per cent wastage.

The total for the UK was £10 billion of food being bought and chucked into the bin each year. It cost another billion pounds for local authorities to collect this and send it to landfill where it generated 18 million tonnes of CO_2. If that CO_2 was eliminated it would be about the same as taking one in every five cars off the road.

Since those 30 billion food miles they talk about us generating in the UK are responsible for nearly 19 million tonnes of carbon dioxide production annually, by eliminating this waste we would reduce our national emissions by a further 6 million tonnes or so. That's got to take a few lorries off the road as well.

One answer that local authorities have come up with, faced as they are with increasing costs and penalties for landfill, is to separate food waste and use it in biodigesters. There it generates a little electricity and is processed into compost.

Farmers grow our food, which is processed and packaged. Then it is distributed to warehouses and shops where we buy it, only to bin it, then to be transported to a biodigester. So it is fairly obvious that cutting out this food waste makes absolute sense environmentally as well as economically.

We've nearly eliminated food waste in our house. One by-product of growing your own is that you appreciate the real value of food, which is what started us down this road of stopping waste. The first thing is not to buy food you don't need. It may seem obvious, but many people buy the same things each week regardless of what's left from the week before.

Keep an eye on what is in your fridge. If you find you have something you are not going to eat before it goes out of date, change your plans and use it up or freeze it if possible. Freezing stops the clock, but don't forget you will restart the clock when you defrost it. Remember that if you have defrosted something, never just refreeze it. It's perfectly safe, however, to defrost something, cook it and then freeze the cooked food.

On the subject of 'plate waste', use serving bowls rather than dish out everything onto the plate. Make it a family rule that you eat what goes onto the plate so that leftovers are nice and clean in the serving dishes.

If there's only a few vegetables left, pop them into a bag and freeze. When you've got a reasonable amount in the freezer you can add it to a stock or soup. Larger amounts can go into a Tupperware-type container and into the fridge for tomorrow's meal.

A slice of beef or pork from the joint will make a nice sandwich for the next day's lunch, but if you've enough for another meal then a curry or sweet and sour can be made. OK, the super chefs who write cookbooks will recoil in horror, but you can make a perfectly palatable dinner with already cooked meat. If it's summer, then just slice the meat thinly and it's the basis for a salad. Be creative. It's sinful to waste meat that an animal died to provide you with.

Here are a few of our 'waste not, want not' recipes to use up the remains of a Sunday joint.

'Waste not, want not' recipes

Hot and spicy pork

This will serve four. If you have less pork available, make up the weight with mushrooms.

Ingredients

2tbsp vegetable oil

450g (1lb) pork, cut into thin strips

1 or 2 cloves of garlic, crushed

1 red pepper, seeded and cut into thin strips

1 green pepper, seeded and cut into thin strips (in the winter we pull out a 'pack' of our own peppers that have been prepared and frozen)

1tbsp chilli sauce or 1 or 2 dried chilli peppers (our own), crushed and finely chopped (no need to remove the seeds)

1tsp white wine vinegar

1tsp sugar (demerara works best)

1tbsp light soy sauce

300ml (½ pint) chicken stock (preferably home-made)

salt and pepper to taste

1 or 2tsp cornflour to thicken

Method

- Heat the oil in a wok or large frying pan.
- Stir in the pork, garlic and peppers and cook for 2 or 3 minutes until browned.
- Pour off any excess oil, add the chilli sauce or dried peppers, vinegar, sugar, soy sauce and chicken stock. Season with salt and pepper.
- Cook for about 10 minutes, then thicken the sauce with the cornflour mixed with a little water.
- Continue cooking until the sauce is nice and thick and reduced slightly.
- Serve hot with long-grain rice or plain noodles.

Beef curry or korma

I was amazed to learn that some people we know throw away leftover beef from the Sunday joint. Why? It's cooked and perfectly safe for a few days in the fridge. Here's what we often do with it:

Ingredients

vegetable oil, ghee or butter (just enough for frying)

1 largish onion, peeled and chopped

2 largish cloves of garlic, crushed

450g (1lb) beef or 225g ($^{1}/_{2}$lb) beef and 112g ($^{1}/_{4}$lb) chopped mushrooms

curry spices to your taste (I go for mild or korma mix)

1 standard tin (400g) chopped tomatoes*, plus enough water to fill the empty can

cream or evaporated milk (optional)

* We don't use tinned tomatoes. When we have the tomato glut in August we pop them into boiling water, remove their skins, zap through a blender and freeze. That way we've always got tomatoes for cooking.

Method

● Heat the oil, ghee or butter and add the onion, crushed garlic, beef and/or mushrooms and fry gently. Add the curry spices to taste and continue stirring until the ingredients are well coated and the spices have infused the contents with their flavour.

- Add the tomatoes and water, stir until it comes to the boil and then reduce the heat and simmer gently for at least an hour.
- By this time the curry should have reduced considerably and have a thick consistency. At this time add a little cream or evaporated milk if you like it creamy and continue to cook for a short while.
- Serve with basmati rice and your favourite pickles and chutneys.

Making the most of poultry

Poultry used to be quite an expensive meat but now, thanks to industrial battery methods, chicken is as cheap as chips and we treat it with contempt. If you share an uneasiness in eating food produced by cruelty, but don't have money to waste, then getting the most from your bird is paramount.

Generally, the most cost-effective way to buy any chicken (or other poultry for that matter) is as a whole bird. Buying drumsticks or thighs or breasts is another way the producers 'add value', and value in this context equals value to them and cost to you.

Having said that, if you're living on your own, then it can make sense to buy a breast or a small pack of drumsticks. However, there is nothing to stop you buying a whole bird, jointing it and freezing what you don't need immediately.

If you roast a chicken and serve the breast and legs, there's still a lot of meat on the bones. When it's cooled down, take the carcase and pick it over. Turn it upside down and you'll find some delicious pieces of meat under the skin. Strip the meat from the wings and thighs as well as any left on the main carcase. If there's not enough left to do anything with today, freeze it to add to another load and make up enough for a meal. You might make a chicken soup or even a chicken and ham pie – effectively with free chicken that many people just throw away.

I hope you didn't throw away those bones and bits of skin. They will make a delicious stock you can use in any recipe that calls for it, but is especially good for soups. We never seem to have enough stock in stock (sorry, I couldn't resist that!) so Oxo cubes get used for gravies, but the real stock is reserved for soups.

Stock is so easy; just break up the carcase and put it in a large saucepan with the chicken skin and bits along with a chopped-up onion, chopped clove of garlic, a carrot and other veggies. Some of your frozen leftover vegetables will do just fine. A couple of bay leaves go well if you have them.

Add about half a teaspoon of salt and the same of ground pepper, then simmer for a couple of hours. If you've got a pressure cooker, you can achieve the same result in just 40 minutes at full pressure.

Allow it to cool and then strain the liquid into jugs. Check over the bones and remove any bits of meat. You can pop these along with the veggies into a blender and liquidise with some of the stock. Add it to the jugs and put them into the fridge for a while. As the stock cools, the fat floats to the top and you can discard it.
(I know, one day we'll work out a way to run cars on it ... but not just yet.)

Your stock can now be frozen until required. If this all seems a bit time-consuming, there's nothing to stop you breaking up and freezing the carcase and then batch cooking a couple in one go.

Another way we handle a whole chicken is to make a variant on coq-au-vin.

Our creamy coq-au-vin

Ingredients

1 onion, finely chopped

3–5 cloves of garlic (according to taste), crushed

vegetable oil (preferably olive) and butter (just enough for frying)

225g (½lb) smoked streaky bacon, cut into chunks (you could substitute lardons)

1 chicken, jointed

500ml (1pt) chicken stock (made from stock cubes is fine)

500ml (1pt) cheap red wine

450g (1lb) button mushrooms, or value mushrooms, cut into chunks

herbs (thyme goes well, and a bayleaf, but don't worry if you don't have any)

salt and pepper

cream (double, single or whatever comes to hand)

Method

- Soften the onion and garlic in the oil and butter in a large pan. Add the streaky bacon and fry for a minute and then add the jointed chicken.

- Add the stock and red wine. Bring to the boil and then reduce the heat to a slow simmer.
- Add the mushrooms and herbs and seasoning.
- After 45–60 minutes, the chicken will be falling off the bone.
- Remove the chicken and pour off enough of the liquid to make a sauce – usually just over a pint, say 600ml, is enough – into another pan. Add some cream to taste and thicken. If it's too runny, mix a teaspoon of cornflour with milk and whisk this into the sauce.
- Enjoy your meal and then strip the meat off the leftover chicken pieces and add to the leftover sauce. Whizz this in a food processor and you now have the basis for a rich chicken soup. Either keep in the fridge for the next day or freeze for later. Just warm up and add cream to whiten before serving; if it is too rich, thin down with skimmed milk. This uses nigh on every bit of the chicken and will provide the basis of two nutritious and tasty meals for four people.

Jointing a chicken

Since jointing a chicken seems to be almost a lost skill, here is how to do it. You can use a sharp knife but I find some heavy kitchen scissors easiest for parts of this job.

- Snip off the parson's nose and the ends of the legs and wings.
- Cut tight along one side of the breast bone through the ribs, opening the bird out.
- Cut off the legs and thighs, trying to ensure there's a fair chunk of meat attached to each.
- Cut the legs at the joint into two.

You've now got eight meal-sized pieces and the base of the carcase. The diagram below should make things clear.

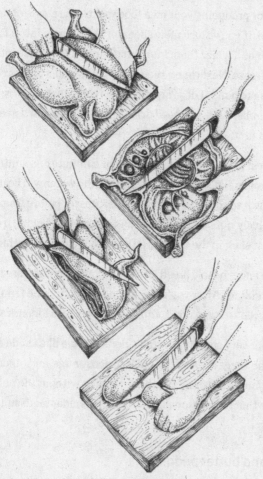

Fig. 2. Jointing a chicken.

Making your own bread

Once you make your own bread, you'll find that throwing away stale bread is something you don't want to do. It's amazing how growing or producing your own food makes you aware of its real value. If you've just a few slices left, drop them into a food processor and whizz them into breadcrumbs. Pop these into a bag and freeze. Next time a recipe calls for breadcrumbs you have them to hand. These are fine for a recipe that calls for fresh breadcrumbs, but if you need dried breadcrumbs you'll need to dry the bread first.

The easiest method is to microwave for a minute or so until the bread is steaming, which means most of the water will be driven out. Allow it to cool and whizz in the processor before freezing. Alternatively, cut into thin slices and spread on a baking tray on the lowest shelf in the oven when you are cooking something else.

If you've enough stale bread left, then why not make a bread and butter pudding? After you've made one, you'll find the family hiding bread so it goes stale and you've an excuse for another!

This is our very easy basic recipe. Some people like to add candied peel, some slices of dried fruit like apricot or figs, and others like cinnamon. We prefer the basic version without the nutmeg, although that is traditional. Like all recipes, adapt it to suit your tastes.

Bread and butter pudding

Don't bother buying caster sugar; just put ordinary cheap white sugar into a grinder and whizz for a few seconds.

If you use skimmed or semi-skimmed milk, add a little cream or mix a tablespoon of dried milk powder into the milk to add a little body.

Ingredients

6 or so thinly cut slices of bread, buttered on both sides

100g (4oz) currants and/or sultanas

2 eggs

600ml (1 pint) full cream milk

50g (2oz) caster sugar

nutmeg, grated (if you like it)

Method

● Grease a pie dish and arrange the bread and butter slices in it, sprinkling on the fruit as you go.

● Beat the eggs and add the milk and sugar, then pour into the pie dish. Leave to stand for 15 minutes, then grate some nutmeg onto the top.

● Place into a very cool oven (Gas Mark 1/275°F/140°C) for 1¹/₄ hours until the custard is set.

CHAPTER FIVE

Storing vegetables

If you grow your own, then you are going to need to address where you store your harvest bounty. The kitchen cupboard may cope with a bag of potatoes, but it isn't the right place to keep half a dozen sacks.

Although a freezer is great for keeping many vegetables in good condition from harvest to when they are needed, freezers are not really ideal or necessary for crops such as potatoes, root crops or onions, and so on. Root crops particularly are ideal for storing. After all, nature designed them for this purpose!

In days of old, root crops would be stored in a clamp outdoors which worked quite well for bulk storage, but clamps are not the best method for storing the smaller amounts required by a small family or couple. Clamps were also quite vulnerable to vermin, and building them properly and making them weatherproof required skill. Nowadays the farmers store their produce in climate-controlled facilities at the optimum temperature and humidity, safe from vermin.

The best place at home is somewhere cool and dark but not too cold. A garage is often ideal, especially one attached or integral to the house. (How often do people actually keep a car in there?) Another option is a garden shed. The only problem is that sheds do tend to vary in temperature. In the winter they can drop almost as low as the outside temperature (and you don't want to freeze your food store), while on a sunny spring day the temperature will shoot right up.

It's easy enough to insulate your shed. Polystyrene is a good insulator and you can often pick up sheets used for packaging for the price of asking from electrical goods' retailers. Large and thicker sheets can be bought cheaply from builders' merchants.

You do need some ventilation to prevent condensation building up. Closable air vent covers can be useful for this and can be picked up very cheaply from builders' merchants. Ideally you want to keep the temperature above freezing in cold weather, so a thermostatically controlled heater is useful. If you keep your storage area small (we walled off and shelved a section of our large shed to become the food store), then it isn't expensive to run.

Another solution we came up with was a 60-watt light bulb in an old biscuit tin with holes punched through, which we ran at night. It made a very low wattage electric heater, enough to keep the frost off. However, soon you will not be able to buy old-fashioned, high-energy light bulbs any more.

If you haven't got electricity, then it gets trickier. A paraffin heater is cheap to run but produces condensation, something you definitely don't want. You can buy thermostatic-controlled tent heaters or even a camping stove turned down to its lowest, but be really careful with naked flames. You don't want to burn down your shed (and I think they might produce condensation as well).

When storing vegetables you need to sort out the damaged ones and any showing signs of rot and use these first. The phrase 'One bad apple spoils the barrel' is very apt. One rotten potato can spoil the sack very quickly. Blight, in particular, spreads like wildfire, turning a sack into a stinking soggy mess in a couple of weeks.

Potatoes

We'll start with this staple that provides such an important part of our diet. When you first harvest your potatoes leave them out in the sun for a few hours to dry off and allow the skin to harden a little. After this, brush off any excess soil and check for damage. Sometimes it is hard to tell. As a little hole on the surface can indicate a network of tunnels and even a live slug hiding in the potato, check as carefully as you can, putting any seconds to one side to be used first.

The most important thing to do is to exclude light. Prolonged exposure to light will cause greening of the potato. Green potatoes are poisonous as it indicates that solanine, an alkaloid, has been formed. Remember that potatoes are part of the same family (*Solanaceae*) as deadly nightshade! Partially green potatoes are still edible – just cut off the affected parts. You can often reverse the problem by keeping green potatoes in total darkness for a few weeks.

You can store potatoes in paper sacks, often available for the asking at chip shops, but leave the neck slightly open to allow excess moisture to escape. Damp or wet potatoes will rot quickly so do not use plastic bags under any circumstances as they hold the moisture in. The best container is a hessian sack. You can buy these quite easily and many potato suppliers sell them as well. They can be washed and reused, so will last for a few years.

Unlike other root crops, potatoes should preferably be stored above 5°C (41°F), as below that the starch turns into sugars, which can give them a strange sweet taste. The optimum storage temperature range is 5–10°C (41–50°F). If you do find they've got too cold and developed a sweet taste, bring them into the warm for a week before using.

After the potatoes have been in store for a month or so, wait for a fine day and empty the bags out. Check for developing rots and don't be surprised if you find the odd slug or two you missed first time round. I pop a few slug pellets into the sack as there is always one you miss.

Your potatoes will store quite well until the spring when they start to sprout. Just knock these sprouts off before peeling. With luck, you should have edible potatoes in store until your new potatoes arrive in late spring, early summer.

Other root crops

You can store other root crops, including carrots, parsnips and beetroot, in the following way. Remove foliage close to the crown. Place in layers in boxes or crates, separated with damp, but not wet, packing material. You can use sand, coir or even leaf mould, but probably the best is peat. (Before the fundamentalist wing of the organic movement issues a reward for my capture, dead or alive, I would point out that peat used as a packing material can be reused year after year and you can buy peat filtered from water, which is totally sound ecologically.)

The best type of box we have found is the banana box. Most supermarkets throw them away and will give you some if you ask. They're actually great when you move house as well!

The ideal temperature for your root crops is between 0 and 4°C (32 and 39.2°F) – lower than potatoes – but it isn't that critical. Since you probably don't have a refrigerated warehouse storage facility, you will just have to settle for the coolest place available.

If you wish you can leave parsnips in the ground through the winter, digging up as required. In fact parsnips taste better when they've had a few frosts, so don't be in too much of a hurry to harvest them. They do want to be up before spring arrives though, as they'll start to regrow and produce seed heads, ruining them as a crop.

Onions

To store well, your onions need to be properly dried out (more difficult with large onions). Resist the urge to dry them out somewhere too warm. I used a greenhouse one year and one sunny day filled the air with the aroma of cooking onions. An expensive lesson as we lost the crop.

Once dried, you then trim the roots about 1cm ($\frac{1}{2}$in) from the base and the leaves to about 22cm (9in), then string them to hang up in a cool dry place until required. Stringing onions is easy when you get the hang of it.

- Take a length of string and double it.
- Next make a loop at the base and feed the neck of the first onion into that.
- Hang the string from a nail to continue, it's a lot easier.
- The onion leaves are threaded through the double rope and the next is threaded in the opposite direction, alternating until your string is full. Through, around and down is what we repeat to keep the technique in mind.

The diagram on page 56 should explain the process.

Garlic and shallots

Both of these store well and although the 'correct' method is to braid them like onions, it's a very fiddly job. The easy way is just to let them dry off and then store in net bags hung from the wall in a dark place with good ventilation. The legs of ladies' tights and stockings make great storage nets. Don't put too many in one net or the lack of airflow will encourage rot.

Marrows, squashes, pumpkins and tight-headed cabbage

All of these will store well. We've had butternut squash keep for six months, although that was unusual. Once again you want somewhere cool and dark with good ventilation. Slatted shelves are ideal as these allow the air to get around them. Don't overcrowd or you will encourage still air and rots.

With cabbages there is always the problem of little slugs inside. Take the outer leaves off down to a clean tight centre and most should be dealt with. Rubbing a little salt on the outside helps as well.

Once cut, your cabbage will not keep well but, if you wrap it tightly with cling film and put it into the fridge, you can have perfectly edible fresh cabbage for up to a month.

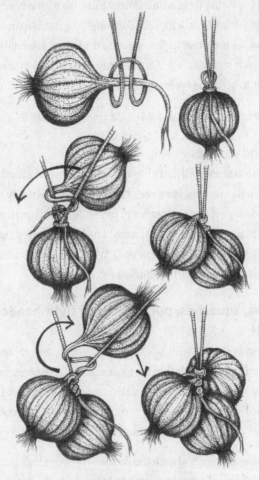

Fig. 3. Stringing onions.

CHAPTER SIX
Storing and preserving food

In years gone by, people were far more dependent on the season. When a crop finished, that was it until next year. The space between the last crops of one year and the new crops of the next is still called 'the hungry gap'.

That's the reason we had and still have our main feast of the year at midwinter. By Christmas many of the last crops were deteriorating badly and it was eat them or lose them. The excess animals would have been slaughtered, just leaving the breeding stock for next year, and so a surplus of fresh meat was there to be eaten as well.

Of course, some crops could be stored. Grains kept well and were ground into flour as needed for the daily bread. Peas and beans would have been dried and root crops such as carrots and parsnips stored in clamps. Meat and fish would be dried, smoked and salted down. With luck and a good year's bounty, there would be enough to last until the next season.

The really wealthy, the aristocracy (who today would be multi-millionaires), could afford to build ice houses and pay for ice to be cut from frozen ponds to keep some foods in fair condition. It's really hard for us to imagine how difficult just keeping starvation at bay was for the ordinary person until relatively recently. When sugar became a common product, imported from the colonies and produced by slaves, a new method of keeping the summer bounty for the winter became possible: jams and chutneys, which depend on sugar as a preservative.

From the 1850s a large industry developed in supplying ice. Incredibly, large ships would sail from the north to the warmer south with cargo holds full of ice where it would be unloaded to store in ice houses and then cut into chunks to be sold to wealthy, middle-class households. The ice would be used to power an appliance similar to a modern refrigerator.

By the 1930s the icebox and ice industry were mainly replaced by modern refrigerators but, although these were cheaper than the icebox to run, they were still a luxury. Pre-war houses often incorporated a pantry with a marble slab shelf. This was to help keep foods cool, but was hardly effective and safe by our modern standards.

It wasn't until the 1950s that the fridge was more likely to be found in a kitchen than not. We had to wait for the 1970s before domestic freezers started to be commonplace.

A freezer is essential

Now an efficient freezer can be picked up new cheaply, or second-hand for peanuts. Our strategy for low-cost living absolutely depends on being able to store our home-grown food and bought-in bargains, and the freezer is central to this strategy. While there are other methods of storing and preserving foods (as mentioned above), the fact is that freezing is very easy and safe. Done properly, freezing retains taste, texture and vitamins. Above all, it is quick, which is a real benefit when both partners are working and time is at a premium.

You really want the most efficient freezer you can get to keep the electricity costs to a minimum, and it must be four-star to be able to freeze down food from room temperature.

One question raised frequently is how long items can be stored in a freezer. Food stored constantly at -18°C (-0.4°F) or lower will always be safe. **Note that it must be kept at -18°C or below continuously.** Only the quality of taste and texture can suffer with lengthy freezer storage. Freezing keeps food safe by causing microbes to enter a dormant stage and preserves food for extended periods because it prevents the growth of micro-organisms that cause food spoilage.

Don't forget that once thawed these microbes can again become active and begin multiplying again. Since they will then grow at about the same rate as micro-organisms on fresh food, you must handle thawed items as you would any perishable food.

Our freezer has a guide that states the following storage times for various foods:

- Up to three months for fish, bread, shellfish and cooked dishes.
- Up to six months for egg products, pork, butter and ice cream.
- Up to nine months for mushrooms, lamb, cheese and fruits.
- Up to twelve months for poultry, beef and vegetables.

Any commercial frozen food will have individual guidance for how long it can be stored, and any freezable fresh food will usually give a storage time as well. If you pick up a bargain at the end-of-date life in the supermarket, look for that magic 'freezable' symbol before stocking up.

Our experience is that hard cheese like Cheddar can be frozen successfully but it tends to be more crumbly when thawed out (still fine for cooking though). Bacon can be frozen, but it seems to develop a strange aftertaste when kept for more than a month. Fish also seems to suffer when stored for too long. Having said that, we enjoyed some trout that had been forgotten for a year and it tasted as good as the day we froze it. We've eaten home-made spaghetti sauce that was two years old and was fine, as well as beef and sweetcorn that were two and three years old respectively.

The best rule is always to take out and eat the oldest food first. However, if you have discovered something lurking under the beans for two years, defrost it and see. The human nose is a remarkable instrument and part of our design is a sensitivity to food that is off. If it smells strange, throw it away – but most often we find that things keep far longer than the official guidance.

Successful freezing depends on how quickly you can reduce the temperature of the food. Slow freezing may not make the food inedible but will affect flavour and, more importantly, nutritional value. Fast freezing halts bacterial growth instantly and produces very small ice crystals, which cause less damage to the cell structure of the food. Slow freezing results in a mushy texture, and the food will often be inedible when defrosted.

Before you commence preparing food for freezing, turn your freezer on to its super or fast setting – preferably 3 hours or so before. Do check the individual appliance's instructions; some machines require longer. This just keeps the motor running and drops the temperature as low as possible. When the food goes into the freezer it will cause the overall temperature to rise as the relatively hot food cools. The super setting ensures the food already there remains at the optimum temperature of -18°C (-0.4°F) and the food being frozen cools as quickly as possible.

Do not try to freeze too much in one go – never more than 10 per cent of the freezer capacity at a time. Also, the colder the food when it goes into the freezer, the less work the freezer has to do. We pre-cool in the fridge down to about 5°C (41°F) before freezing down to -18°C (-0.4°F).

We tend to batch cook. After all, it takes no more energy to use the oven for four lasagnes than for one, or much more time to make enough spaghetti sauce for six meals than for one on the hob. By freezing our own 'ready meals' we save time as well. Do be aware that freezing seems to enhance the effect of seasoning and spices. A hot curry can become quite dramatic when it is defrosted.

You can buy Tupperware-style containers suitable for the freezer cheaply but old margarine tubs and ice-cream cartons can be used. Another good source of freezer containers are those plastic boxes that Chinese takeaways come in now. If you want quite a few, then try asking at a takeaway if they'll sell them to you. They are only pennies to buy.

We mainly use our freezers for our own home-grown produce. Fresh is best, of course, but the fact is you'll always have a glut when home-growing and it is nice to eat your favourites out of season. Some things are unsuitable for freezing such as chicory, cucumber, endive, Jerusalem artichokes, kale, lettuce and radishes. Other vegetables, such as potatoes and other roots, are best stored in other ways (see Chapter 5), but you can freeze them if you wish.

To get your vegetables to store well, you need to blanch them. This is essential with most vegetables. Blanching destroys certain enzymes and bacteria while helping to preserve the colour, texture and flavour of the food. It also helps retain vitamin C.

The method is really quite simple. You need to put the food into boiling water and raise its temperature as fast as possible. We used to use a large jam pan, but we now use a large saucepan with a lid. Even just sitting the lid on the blanching basket reduces the time the water needs to get back up to temperature and the energy needed to maintain it. You need about 4 litres of water per 500g of produce, at least 6 pints to 1lb.

You also need a blanching basket. This is just like a sieve and is used to hold the produce together in the pan and to enable you to lift it out easily when finished.

With water in your pan at a fast boil, put your vegetables in the basket and plunge it into the water. The water needs to be back up to a rolling boil in 1 minute or less. If you can't do that, blanch smaller portions. Keep a lid over the pan to hold the heat and steam in. Then hold at the boil for the time stated below.

After boiling you need to get the temperature down as fast as possible and stop the cooking process. We plunge the basket into a bowl of cold water for 5 seconds or so to kill the heat, then transfer to a second large bowl of water with ice cubes in it, changing the water in the first bowl each time to keep it as cold as possible.

If the boiling blanching water starts looking mucky you should change it. When this happens depends on the vegetable.

When the food is cold, remove from the water and drain and/or dry off – beware: broad beans will turn your tea towel brown! – then pack into portion-sized freezer bags. We tried large bags but the contents tended to stick together and you can always use two smaller bags if you have visitors for a meal.

Pre-chill in the fridge down to 5°C (41°F) to reduce the workload on the freezer and freeze the food faster, then put the food into the freezer. Remember, not too much in one go or the existing contents may rise in temperature and will deteriorate.

Freezing vegetables

Artichokes, globe

Remove all outer coarse leaves and stalks, and trim tops and stems. Wash well in cold water and add a little lemon juice to the blanching water. Blanch a few at a time, in a large container, for 7–10 minutes. Cool, and drain well before freezing.

Asparagus

Grade into thick and thin stems. Wash in cold water and blanch thick stems for about 4 minutes and thin for just 2 minutes. Cool and drain, then tie into small bundles, packed tips to stalks, separated by non-stick paper. Generally asparagus doesn't work too well as a frozen vegetable, so bottling or making into a soup and freezing works best.

Aubergines

Peel and cut roughly into 2.5cm (1in) slices. Blanch for 4 minutes, chill and dry on absorbent paper. Pack in layers, separated by non-stick paper. You can also fry the slices instead of blanching and then freeze. This doesn't work too well, but is usable in a dish like moussaka.

Beans, broad

Mature beans actually seem to benefit from freezing; younger small beans freeze well also. Just shell and blanch for 3 minutes before cooling and freezing.

Beans, French

These always come in flushes so a glut is usual. Most varieties freeze very well but some of the waxier types are better fresh. Just wash, top and tail and then blanch for 2 minutes before chilling and freezing.

Beans, runner

These freeze well. Prepare as you normally would and blanch for 3 minutes before cooling and freezing.

Beetroot

Beetroot is normally stored as for root crops but we like the convenience of being able to take one from the freezer ready prepared for a salad, so we freeze some small beetroot for this. Wash well and rub the skin off after blanching. Small beets up to 7.5cm (3in) in diameter need blanching for 10 minutes and larger beets should be cooked until tender, (45–50 minutes). A pressure cooker will reduce the time and save energy for this.

Freeze the smaller beets whole but slice or dice larger beets or they will take too long to freeze. If you blanch for a shorter time, you will find they are rubbery when defrosted.

Broccoli and calabrese

Trim off any woody parts and large leaves. Wash in salted water, and cut into small sprigs. Blanch thin stems for 3 minutes, medium stems for 4 minutes and thick stems for 5 minutes. Cool and drain well. The thick woody stems and leaves will work well in a soup.

Brussels sprouts

Prepare as you would normally, removing any outer leaves and washing thoroughly. Blanch for 3 minutes, chill and freeze. When you defrost, they're effectively cooked enough so we just toss in melted butter with salt and black pepper until they're warmed through.

Cabbage

You can freeze cabbage but it tends to be soggy when defrosted, so we cook it like Brussels sprouts. Don't forget that a cabbage will store well for several weeks in somewhere cool, dark but airy. You can also wrap it in cling film and keep it in the fridge for a few weeks.

Wash and shred the leaves, then blanch for just a minute before chilling, draining and freezing.

Carrots

Maincrop large carrots are best stored as a root crop but young carrots can be prepared ready, either cut into strips or diced, before blanching for 3 minutes and then chilling and freezing.

With damaged maincrop carrots that will not store well, we cook them in the pressure cooker and then mash with a little salt, too much butter and pepper. This freezes well and can be made 50:50 with swede or parsnips.

Cauliflower

Wash and break into small sprigs, about 5cm (2in) in diameter. Add the juice of a lemon to the blanching water to keep them white; blanch for 3 minutes, cool, drain and pack.

Celeriac

Wash and trim. Cook until almost tender, peel and slice, then freeze when cool.

Courgettes and marrows

Choose young ones. Wash and cut into 1cm (½–1in) slices. Either blanch for 1 minute, or sauté in a little butter. We've found these don't work well but are just about acceptable in a risotto when defrosted.

Fennel

Trim and cut into short lengths. Blanch for 3 minutes, cool, drain and pack.

Kohlrabi

Use small roots, 5–7cm (2–3in) in diameter. Cut off the tops, peel and dice. Blanch for $1^{1}/_{2}$ minutes, cool, drain and pack.

Leeks

Prepare as normal and then slice fairly thinly (less than 2.5cm/1in). Blanch for 2 minutes or sauté in oil. Cool and freeze. They will be soggy when defrosted but fine for adding to casseroles or soups.

Mushrooms

Choose small button mushrooms and leave whole; wipe clean but don't peel. Sauté for a minute in butter or oil. Mushrooms larger than 2.5cm (1in) in diameter are suitable only for slicing and using in cooked dishes.

Onions

Can be peeled, finely chopped and packed in small plastic containers for cooking later; packages should be overwrapped, to prevent the smell filtering out.

Small onions may be blanched whole and used later in casseroles. Blanch sliced onions for 2 minutes, small whole onions for 4 minutes. Usually onions keep well enough so you shouldn't need to freeze them anyway.

Parsnips

Treat just as carrots or cut into chips, blanch for 2 minutes, cool and freeze to make parsnip chips or roasties.

Peas

Process as soon as you can after picking because the sugars are turning into starch when they come off the plant. Shell and put into a pan of cold water. If there are any pea maggots these will float and can be easily fished out. Blanch for a minute or two at most; shake the basket to ensure heat is evenly distributed. We find it easier just to drop loosely into the pan and fish out with a sieve as they go through the holes in the blanching basket anyway. Peas freeze really well.

Older peas can be dried or usefully made into 'mushy peas', which can also be frozen.

Peas, mange-tout

Trim the ends. Blanch for 2 minutes, cool, drain and pack.

Peppers, chilli

Usually we just string and dry chilli peppers but you can freeze them. We had some small round Habeneros that for some reason would go mouldy rather than dry. We halved, deseeded and froze them individually on a tray without blanching before packing into bags. Although freezing usually concentrates spicy flavours, with chilli peppers it seems to make them milder.

Peppers, sweet

These freeze well for cooking but do go a bit soggy for use in a salad. Wash well, remove stems and all traces of seeds and membranes before blanching for 3 minutes as halves for stuffed peppers, or in thin slices for stews and casseroles.

Potatoes

Although normally you would store potatoes in sacks, sometimes you have a glut of damaged potatoes that will not keep too well and freezing, if you have room, avoids wasting them.

They are best frozen in a cooked form, as partially cooked chips (fully cooked ones are not satisfactory), croquettes, mashed or duchesse potatoes. The only method I can recommend as being much good is as chips. Prepare as usual and part fry in deep fat for 2 minutes, cool and freeze, ready for final frying.

Spinach

True spinach (as opposed to beet or perpetual spinach) is another crop that tends to arrive at once. Luckily it goes down an awful lot when blanched so does not take up much room in the freezer. Select young leaves and wash very thoroughly under running water; drain. Blanch for 2 minutes in small quantities, cool quickly and press out excess moisture. Pack in rigid containers or polythene bags, leaving 1cm ($^1/_2$in) headspace.

Sweetcorn

Sweetcorn is one vegetable that is unbeatable when really fresh, but it will store fairly well for up to a week in the fridge. If you are not going to use it before that, then it is best to freeze. Remove husks and 'silks'. Blanch small cobs for 3 minutes, medium ones for 4 minutes and large cobs for 5 minutes in plenty of water. Cool and dry.

You can freeze them whole on the cob or cut off the kernels with a sharp knife and just freeze them in portion bags.

Tomatoes, whole

When the tomato crop comes in we find we're overwhelmed. Although they can be bottled well, it's easiest and fastest just to pop them into a bag and freeze them. They're only useful for cooking after being frozen, but there is a benefit in that the skin comes off very easily when they're defrosted.

Tomato, purée

Skin and core tomatoes; simmer in their own juice for 5 minutes until soft. Pass them through a nylon sieve or, easier still, liquidise and pack in small containers when cool.

Turnips

Use small, young turnips. Trim and peel, then cut into small dice. Blanch for 2 minutes, cool, drain and freeze. Turnips may be fully cooked and mashed before freezing like carrots.

Freezing fruit

Apples

Apples can be bottled or dried, but slices of apple can be blanched for 2 minutes prior to chilling and freezing for later use in pies and flans. If you're worried about them discolouring, soaking in lemon juice for a moment before blanching helps cure this.

Usually we freeze some surplus apples in the form of a purée. Just peel, core and stew with a very small amount of water and sugar to taste in a heavy pan. A knob of butter on the bottom helps stop sticking. Mash with a fork and freeze in portions when cool. These are easy to pull out for apple sauce with a pork meal.

Berries and currants

All the berries, from blackberries and blackcurrants to gooseberries and strawberries, can be frozen. Usually we do this when we're building up enough for a jam-making session as the freezing process makes the fruit soggy and unsuitable for eating fresh.

The easiest way is just to prepare the fruit as if for cooking, removing stalks and hulling strawberries, etc. Then make sure they're dry and spread on a tray and freeze. When frozen pack into bags.

Damsons and plums

Once again the purée method is the best we've found for these. You can also freeze in a syrup. Mix 1lb (450g) sugar with 1 litre (2 pints) water until dissolved. Stone and halve the plums before adding. By adding 200–300mg ascorbic acid (vitamin C) to the syrup you prevent discolouration. It's available quite cheaply as a powder. You only need a third of a gram, so half a teaspoon seems about right.

Pears

Pears just don't seem to work for freezing except as a purée. Even freezing in syrup results in a mush. They're better stored in other ways or turned into perry.

Rhubarb

Rhubarb can be frozen but only for later use in cooking. Wash, trim and cut into 2.5cm (1in) lengths. Blanch for 1 minute, chill and freeze.

Bottling fruit and vegetables

Bottling as a method of storing foods goes right back to the time of the Greeks and Romans. They found that excluding air was a key part of keeping foods edible for a long period. Making a pot or a jar wasn't a problem, but creating an airtight lid was. Various sealing methods were tried, usually involving fat or wax that would create a seal when it cooled and hardened. Even pigs' bladders were soaked and stretched over the top of jars to act as lids when they dried, shrinking tightly in the process.

Sadly their methods were hit and miss. Without any knowledge of bacteria or sterilisation, their preserved foods would often go off and eating them was a game of Russian roulette.

In the mid-nineteenth century the rubber-sealed Kilner and Mason jars were developed, bringing a method of reliably sealing out the air, and bottled foods became a lot easier and, more importantly, safer to produce at home.

Although more difficult than home freezing, bottling is more suitable for some fruits and vegetables, preserving not only colour and flavour (like freezing), but also texture (that freezing can destroy). There are other benefits as well. Bottled foods don't require electricity to keep them frozen and there's no defrosting time when you come to use the food. And don't forget that a jar of bottled fruit makes a great Christmas present.

It's not as popular now as it was years ago, but I noticed recently that every French supermarket has a section where you can buy preserving jars and equipment. Mind you, they don't seem to have much in the way of ready meals on the shelf. Perhaps there's a lesson to be learned there.

We not only bottle foods but also make chutneys, jams and other preserves, and one thing we've noticed is how finding specialist equipment in Britain has become harder over the years. The specialist cook shops seem to charge a fortune. eBay is sometimes a good source but we found that Lakeland has the most reasonable prices. If there isn't a shop near you, they supply mail order via their website (www.lakeland.co.uk).

You don't really need any special equipment to bottle successfully apart from the bottles, although you will find it worth investing in some equipment if you start doing a lot of bottling. A sterilising pan with a false bottom and a thermometer are useful for hob sterilising, but a large preserving pan or a lidless pressure cooker with a wire rack in the base will suffice. A home jam-making thermometer, which reads up to 110°C, is useful, but you can get by without it.

There are a number of ways to bottle fruits and vegetables, but these are the easiest ways for the beginner.

Bottling fruit

We bottle fruits in syrup. This helps to best preserve the colour and flavour. The strength of the syrup depends on the sweetness of the fruit and how it is packed, but as a general rule add 250g sugar to 600ml water (8oz to 1 pint). Ordinary granulated white sugar (the cheapest) is fine but you can use honey or even golden syrup instead, which adds a flavour of its own.

Dissolve the sugar in half the water over a moderate heat and, when the sugar is dissolved, boil for 1 minute. Then add the remainder of the water. Doing it this way saves time in waiting for the syrup to cool sufficiently for use. If the syrup is cloudy, strain it through muslin since clear syrup gives a better finish to the fruit.

The sugar preserves the fruit as it sucks the water out of bacteria through a process called osmosis, effectively drying them out so they can't multiply. Vegetables are usually bottled in brine where the salt solution acts in the same way as the sugar.

There are five methods of processing the bottles: a slow water bath, a quick water bath, a slow oven, a hot oven and a pressure cooker method.

The pressure cooker method is quick and so the most efficient in terms of energy for producing small quantities, and it is suitable for all fruits and vegetables. Ideally you need one of the hi-dome styles of cooker to allow enough headroom. It must have a false bottom, a trivet in the base and variable pressure so you can set it to low. Most pressure cookers are fitted with a weight gauge that is usually measured by the appropriate letter:

- L – Low 5lb
- M – Medium 10lb
- H – High 15lb pressure.

Pack the fruit in warm bottles and fill with boiling syrup to within 1in (25mm) of the rim. Fit rubber rings, lids and clips. If using screw bands, screw on loosely.

Pour 850ml (1½ pints) boiling water into the cooker before inserting the bottles. Put the lid on the cooker, with the vent open, and heat until steam appears. Close the vent and bring the pressure up to Low (L) when steam will start to escape.

The time taken from the start of heating until pressure is reached should be no less than 5 minutes or more than 10 minutes, which takes a bit of judgement. You can try it without the bottles first to gauge how high to turn the heat up.

Most fruits bottled in syrup only need to be held at pressure for a minute, although halved or quartered peaches, pears and apples need to be held for 4 minutes. After the time is up, remove from the heat and allow to cool naturally for 10 minutes before releasing any remaining steam pressure. Tighten loose lids and keep in a dark cupboard until you're ready to use.

Bottling vegetables

Although most vegetables can be bottled in theory, in practice it's tomatoes, which are actually a fruit, that get bottled most often – but not in sugar syrup, obviously. You can bottle with the skins or without, as you prefer. To remove the skins easily from tomatoes, dip in boiling water for 10 seconds or so and you'll find they peel off with no trouble.

Pack tightly into the jar and pour on hot brine to which you have added 50ml lemon juice per litre; then process just like the fruit.

You need to keep them under pressure for 5 minutes. The result, with peeled tomatoes, is like a canned tomato and it does work best with a plum variety like Roma.

Drying food

Drying foods is another ancient method of preservation, applied to everything from peas to meat and fish. The principle is quite simple: removing the moisture from the food prevents the growth of bacteria and moulds. Some things take to drying better than others, but all dried food has to be rehydrated to be edible, so some thinking ahead before cooking is needed.

Although most of us are familiar with dried fruits, which make a fantastic and healthy snack or treat, drying vegetables is not so common nowadays. Yet it is an efficient way of storing a glut or even a bargain bulk buy or find.

We all still commonly use dried herbs, and these are simple to grow at home, even in a pot, and dry for later. It is very useful to have a store of dried herbs in the kitchen. Herbs such as parsley, mint, sage and marjoram are often used in large quantities during cooking and a few jars or bunches of dried herbs are an excellent standby to add flavour to soups, stews, vegetables and salads.

Herbs intended for drying should be gathered on a warm dry day, not after rain, and before the sun has warmed the leaves and begun evaporating the essential oils. Pick just before the plants come into flower, as after flowering the leaves start to toughen up. Pick and process one variety or type of herb at a time.

- Remove any dead or withered leaves.
- Tie in small bunches by the stems and blanch in boiling water for just a few seconds.
- Shake off any excess water and leave to dry, or pat dry on a tea towel or kitchen roll.
- Wrap your herb bunch loosely in muslin and hang up to dry in a warm place, such as over a cooker or in an airing cupboard.

The length of time the herbs will take to dry will vary according to the temperature and the draught. If considerable heat is radiating from the cooker, for example, and there is also a good draught, they may be dry in just a few hours. If left in the airing cupboard, where there is little draught, they may take three to four days. The drying process is complete when the main stems of the herbs crack, rather than bend, and the leaves are brittle.

You can dry your herbs in a microwave if you've nowhere to air-dry them. This is a simple and easy process, but you do need to pay careful attention to what you are doing. Lay down two sheets of absorbent kitchen roll, then add a layer of herbs, then another layer of paper towel. Use the microwave on high for 1 minute then in bursts of 30 seconds, moving the herbs around and checking the dryness frequently. The whole process should take no longer than 3 minutes.

Once dry you can hang them in decorative but useful bunches or, more practically, crush the herbs with a rolling pin, discarding any stalks. If you want to reduce them to a fine powder, sieve them. Store in small airtight containers, well filled to preserve the fragrance. If stored in glass bottles, protect them from the light to conserve the colour.

Air-drying fruit and vegetables is rarely successful. We just don't have the right climate in Britain as they do in sunny Spain or the deserts of Nevada. It's a bit like those solar dryers and cookers you find described on the Internet. I'm sure they're fantastic if you have some hot sun, but that's one year in three for us if we're lucky. The two methods we are left with are oven drying or using a drying box.

Oven drying

The most obvious place for drying food is in the oven but, especially with gas ovens, the heat has to be below that of the lowest regulo setting. If using a gas oven for drying, turn the dial to 0 or $1/4$ – the lowest flame possible. It will probably also be necessary to prop open the oven door. This also assists the drying process as adequate ventilation is necessary to remove the moisture as it is driven out of the fruit and vegetables. This also applies to electric ovens, although the temperature is easier to gauge.

With a solid-fuel or oil-fired oven like an Aga or Rayburn, the heat maintained after cooking sessions can be utilised. This may mean that the drying process is not continuous and has to be carried out over several days, but this should not affect the quality of the finished product. Use the simmering oven in solid-fuel cookers for drying, and do allow for adequate ventilation.

The problem with leaving a working oven door open is if you have young children or pets. There's an obvious danger, and with our curious cats it's a non-starter.

When drying either fruit or vegetables in the oven, check the temperature occasionally during the process. It can be very hard to check such low temperatures, even with an oven thermometer, but a guide to the right temperature is to put your ungloved hand in the oven – you should be able to keep it there in comfort for at least 30 seconds.

Drying cabinet

You can buy purpose-made dehydrators, and very effective they are too. Usually they consume around 600 watts when working and incorporate thermostats and timers to enable you to get the perfect result on multiple tray levels (according to the accompanying booklet).

They cost around £100, but I've seen them from £30 second-hand to well over £200. You can also build yourself an effective drying cabinet for under £10. I suspect you can guess our choice.

Use a large wooden or cardboard box and completely seal it except for a few holes in the sides towards the bottom and at the top to allow ventilation. Obviously, some sort of 'door' needs to be allowed for placing whatever you are drying inside.

An electric heat source is also needed. We found the heat from a 60-watt light bulb gave the right temperature for a box of about 75 × 45cm (2$^{1}/_{2}$ × 1$^{1}/_{2}$ ft). The bulb needs to go in the bottom, protected from any dripping juices by a perforated piece of wood or cardboard suspended above it.

Ventilation is important so that the warm air can circulate freely. The food should be placed on either perforated trays, trays or racks with wooden slats and a cheesecloth or muslin base. Wire cake trays or weldmesh cut to size with cheesecloth or muslin stretched over them and fastened at the corners with pins can also be used. This stops the imprint of the wire from marking the fruit or vegetable.

If new cheesecloth or muslin is used, wash and dry before use or it could give the food an unpleasant flavour.

Unlike the shop-bought dryers, you need to use your judgement as to when things are ready.

Fig. 4. A home made dryer.

CHAPTER SEVEN

Making your own chutneys and jams

There's something uniquely satisfying about opening a jar of your own jam or chutney. You know exactly what has gone into the jar, and that nothing from a shop shelf will taste quite the same. Home-made preserves also make a low-cost but very much appreciated gift.

Chutneys add zest to any dish

Chutneys originated in India – the name derives from the Hindi word *chatni* – and the flavours and methods came over to Britain from the Raj in pre-Victorian times. Although we tend to think of chutney as a condiment, a way of adding spice to a dish or a sandwich, it used to be an equal partner in a meal. Bread, ham and the vegetables in piccalilli would form a reasonably balanced and flavoursome meal.

They are made from fruits or vegetables (or a mixture of the two) which are chopped and then cooked, mixed with spices, vinegar and other ingredients to both flavour and preserve.

Windfall apples, green tomatoes and other end-of-season fruit such as rhubarb that would be unsuitable for jam making or bottling can be used as there is no worry about the setting qualities or appearance. This is a distinct advantage for low-cost living. Chutneys are a great way to turn second-class constituents into a first-class product.

The scope of chutneys is endless and the combinations and permutations can be varied according to personal taste and the ingredients available. The end result can be sweet, sour, searingly hot or mild; it all depends on what you want. Another useful feature is that you can substitute easily in chutney recipes; if you don't have one vegetable you just use another.

As well as for your own store cupboard, chutneys make great presents. We usually give our preserves and jams as Christmas presents to friends. One year finances were particularly good so we decided to buy presents from the shops instead. We thought our friends would all be pleased with 'proper' gifts. Well, they all looked slightly disappointed and asked if we'd stopped making things.

One question we're often asked is, 'How long will chutney keep for?' That's not an easy question to answer. In these days where everything bought to eat comes with a use by date, people tend to expect one on a jar of home-made products too. Chutneys certainly need at least a couple of months for the flavours to mature and develop, a little like wine.

We've happily eaten and survived chutney that was over three years old. Obviously to keep well and safely, it's important to maintain a high standard of cleanliness in the kitchen and to ensure jars are properly sterile and the lids are on securely. I was even asked if chutney with mould on the top was safe to eat. If you open a jar and see mould or it smells strange, then don't eat it. It seems obvious to me that common sense isn't so common at times.

You don't need a lot of equipment to make chutneys. The main item is a stainless steel or enamel-lined pan that is large enough to contain all the ingredients. (If you're also a big jam maker it may be well worth investing in a proper preserving pan.) Brass, copper or iron pans should not be used as they react with the vinegar and give a metallic flavour to the chutney.

You'll need a long-handled wooden spoon – this should be reserved for chutney making only as the wood becomes impregnated with the spiciness of the ingredients and could taint other recipes.

Muslin or cotton squares to tie up whole spices needed for flavouring are useful, and some scales to weigh things out. Otherwise everything you need should be found in the kitchen anyway.

To keep your chutney you are going to need heatproof glass jars of assorted sizes. These should be clean, dry, sterilised and warm before use. To sterilise the jars just before filling, put into a cool oven (Gas Mark 1/275°F/140°C) for a few minutes.

The covers for the jars are most important. Vinegar corrodes metal, so use plastic screw or snap-on covers, or metal lids with a plastic preserving skin on the inside surface. Specialist preserving or bottling jars are suitable, either with screw-on or clip-on lids, provided that the lid is made of glass.

Finally, don't forget some labels. We use ordinary printer labels designed for parcels and then create fancy designs on the computer. All that's really important is the contents and date, but gifts look better with a fancy label.

You'll be adding vinegar, sugar and spices to the fruit and vegetables in your chutney. Vinegar is one of the most important ingredients in successful chutney making. It must be of good quality and have an acetic content of at least 5 per cent. Malt, white, wine or cider vinegar can be used, but check the acetic content. Low levels will mean the chutney will not keep.

Sugar can be granulated white or brown. Brown sugar is often preferred as it gives a darker colour to the chutney. Prolonged cooking of any sugar does, however, have a darkening effect, and if a lighter colour is wanted the sugar should only be added when the fruit and/or vegetables are already soft and mushy.

Generally, whole spices are preferable to ground ones which can give a muddy appearance to the chutney. Bruise these and tie them up in a muslin bag and cook with the other ingredients. However, some recipes call for a mixture of both whole and ground spices to give the best flavour.

Never be afraid to experiment. If you like hot flavours add more chilli pepper; if not, use less. Some things work better than others, but remember you are making something to please your palette. Factory-made chutneys are made to recipes that please most people the best. You can create what you think is perfect and, of course, unique.

Sometimes things go wrong. If liquid has collected on top of the chutney it has not been cooked sufficiently. It may be possible to rescue it by tipping it back into the pan, bringing it to the boil again and cooking until the liquid disappears. However, if the chutney has shrunk in the jar, the cover is not airtight and moisture has evaporated. Generally you should write that off.

Here are a couple of easy recipes to get you started from my wife, Val. There are many more recipes and in-depth information, tips and advice in our book *Easy Jams, Chutneys and Preserves*, published by Robinson.

We grow a lot of tomatoes and inevitably we have a lot of green tomatoes at the end of the season. Although you can ripen them indoors, this chutney takes priority. The chutney itself makes a good cooking ingredient. Chicken breasts cooked in green tomato chutney with rice makes a great easy meal.

Val's recipe for green tomato chutney

Makes about 6lb (3kg).

Ingredients

2.25kg (5lb) green tomatoes, washed and chopped finely

500g (1lb) onions, peeled and chopped finely

25g (1oz) salt

250g (8oz) seedless raisins

250g (8oz) sultanas

25g (1oz) root ginger

4 red chillies

1tbsp whole black peppercorns

12 cloves

600ml (1 pint) malt vinegar

500g (1lb) demerara sugar

Method

- Place the tomatoes and onions in a bowl, sprinkle with salt and leave for at least an hour.
- Transfer into a pan with the raisins and sultanas. Bruise the ginger and chillies and put with the other spices into a piece of muslin, tie firmly and add to the pan with the vinegar.
- Bring to the boil and then switch down to a simmer. Add the sugar, stirring frequently until dissolved.
- Continue stirring occasionally and press onto the muslin bag until thickened.

- Remove the muslin bag, which can be reused but not the contents.
- Pour into hot sterilised jars and seal.

Piccalilli

Piccalilli dates right back to the middle of the eighteenth century, with the first recorded recipes being for 'Indian Pickle or Piccalillo' in 1747. Just like that most famous 'traditional' British dish, chicken tikka masala, piccalilli is unique to Britain, using vegetables unknown in India at the time. We're good at absorbing and recreating other cuisines in this country.

There's no absolute right way to make piccalilli; our own recipe varies according to what we have available. Romanesco works well in place of the 'traditional' cauliflower.

A combination of most vegetables can be used for piccalilli, but root vegetables don't tend to work very well. Pick from cauliflower, crisp cabbage, celery, cucumber, courgettes, French and young runner beans, green tomatoes, marrow, peppers, pickling onions, shallots and sweetcorn kernels. These need to be cut into fairly small pieces (1.25–2.5cm/$^{1}/_{2}$–1in).

This recipe makes 1.4–1.8kg (3–4lb) of hot piccalilli.

Ingredients
1.4kg (3lb) prepared mixed vegetables

225g ($^{1}/_{2}$lb) salt

570ml (1 pint) white distilled vinegar

2tsp turmeric

4tsp dry mustard

4tsp ground ginger

84g (3oz) white granulated sugar

14g ($\frac{1}{2}$oz) cornflour

Method

- Put the vegetables in a bowl in alternate layers with the salt and leave overnight.
- Rinse in cold water and drain thoroughly.
- Put most of the vinegar into a pan, add the spices and sugar and bring to the boil.
- Add the vegetables and simmer the mixture until the vegetables are still crisp.
- Blend the cornflour with the remaining vinegar and stir into the vegetable mixture.
- Boil for 2–3 minutes, stirring gently.
- Pack the vegetables into hot, clean sterilised jars* using a slotted spoon.
- Top up with any remaining sauce.
- Cover and seal immediately.
- Label once fully cool.

*It's better to use wide-necked jars like the 450g (1lb) Kilner type as packing narrow jars can get a bit messy!

The joy of home-made jam

Another way to hold onto the summer's bounty is through jam making. In these days of diets and healthy living, jams have taken a bit of a beating. It's true they contain a lot of sugar, which is what preserves the fruit, but a little of what you fancy does no harm.

The main reason for making your own jam has to be the quality and taste. I must admit it has been a long time since we bought jam, but the last time I tasted shop-bought jam it was from one of those fancy little jars in a hotel. I quickly remembered why we bother to make our own.

Jams are extremely versatile and have many uses. As well as accompanying bread and butter, they can be used in home-made scones, pancakes, fillings for sponge cakes, biscuits, steamed puddings, baked puddings, trifles and ice cream to name a few.

Like chutneys, jams and marmalades make great presents or swapping stock for a bit of friendly barter. They're a good way to handle a glut or a bargain buy. I have a particular passion for strawberry jam, with our own strawberries of course, but they tend to trickle in rather than arrive in one large flush for jam making. No matter, just freeze the strawberries until you have enough. They're not good for fresh eating when defrosted, but fine for jam.

You don't need to go out and buy loads of equipment; a large saucepan is fine, although a proper preserving pan makes the job a little easier. We got by for years without a jam thermometer, but eventually went mad and spent a couple of pounds on one.

If you're short of jars, ask a few people to save them for you. If they've tasted your jam, I promise they'll make the effort and remember to keep them for you.

Your two main ingredients are sugar and fruit. Although you can buy special jam sugar, generally we just use ordinary white sugar. We found one of the supermarkets stocks large 8kg bags, saving on the ordinary 1kg price.

The fruit should be dry, sound and not overripe. Fruit which is wet or damaged will cause the jam to go mouldy, and overripe fruit lacks pectin and acid which is also required so the jam will not set properly. Pectin is the substance that works with the sugar to make the jam set. It occurs naturally in some fruits, but if you make a jam with fruits low in pectin such as blackberries or cherries you can buy it from most shops.

The fruit should be thoroughly softened by simmering to extract the pectin. If the sugar is added before the fruit is properly cooked, the jam will not set, the skin of the fruit becomes tough and the jam is often a dark colour.

The general method for making jam is as follows:

- Wash the fruit, drain well and remove the stalks and any stones before weighing. Put into a preserving pan or large saucepan with the water and acid (such as lemon juice) if used, then simmer gently until the fruit is soft.
- Test for pectin content before the sugar is added to the cooked fruit by taking 1tsp juice from the fruit and putting it into a glass and leaving to cool. Add 3tsp of methylated spirit and stir. If a large clot forms in the juice, adequate pectin has been extracted and the sugar may be added. If there is a medium amount of pectin, several small clots will form: you may need to cook for longer or add pectin. If there is very little pectin

content it will break into small pieces and pectin will have to be added.

- Away from the heat, add the warmed sugar and stir until it has dissolved. Return to the heat and bring to the boil, then boil rapidly, stirring occasionally to prevent the jam sticking to the bottom of the pan and burning.

- Remove the pan from the heat and test for setting point by one of the following ways:

  - Put 1tsp jam onto a cold saucer and allow to cool for a minute. Push the surface gently with your fingertip and, if the surface wrinkles, setting point is reached.

  - Dip a wooden spoon into the jam, remove it, and after a second or two tilt the spoon so that the jam drips. If the jam is almost set and the drops run together in large flakes, setting point has been reached.

  - Dip a sugar thermometer in hot water, stir the jam, then immerse the thermometer into it. Do not allow the bulb to touch the bottom of the pan as it may break. If the temperature is around 105°C (220°F) setting point has been reached.

- Add a knob of butter or a few drops of glycerine to the jam, stir well to remove the scum and then immediately pour into clean, sterilised, hot dry jars, filling to within ¼ in (6mm) of the top.

- You should really put a waxed paper circle, waxed side down, over the jar but we just use jars with lids. Wipe clean and leave to cool and then label with contents and date. Store in a cool, dark place.

Once you've got to grips with jams, you can expand your repertoire and include marmalades, conserves, curds and fruit cheeses. After Christmas is a great time to grab some bargain tangerines and make marmalade.

To get you started, here's a recipe for strawberry jam. This makes around 6lb but, if you want, you can halve the amounts.

Strawberry jam

Ingredients
1.8kg (4lb) strawberries

2 lemons, juice

1.8kg (4lb) sugar

Method
- Hull the strawberries, wash and drain well.
- Put into a preserving pan or large saucepan with the lemon juice.
- Simmer gently until the fruit is soft.
- Test for pectin as described above.
- Add the sugar, stirring until it has dissolved.
- Bring to the boil and boil rapidly for 5–10 minutes until the jam sets when tested.
- Remove the scum and leave to cool slightly so that the fruit will not rise in the jars.
- Pot and seal while still warm.

CHAPTER EIGHT

Baking your own bread

The American TV chef Julia Child once said, 'How can a nation be great if their bread tastes like Kleenex?', which sums it up for me. It's the staple food found in every kitchen, so why settle for second best?

Why bake your own bread?

You may wonder why it is worth going to the bother of making your own bread. After all, it's a commodity product that's normally available at a discounted price in the supermarket, and 'end of day' bargain shoppers will usually be able to stock up with loaves reduced to just pennies as they reach the end of their shelf life.

Bread is one of our staple foods, and the supermarkets try to keep the price as low as possible since bread is an item that is easily compared from shop to shop. All loaves in the UK are sold in multiples of 400g, a small loaf being 400g and a large loaf 800g.

However, there has been a small consumer revolt against this industrially produced 'plastic' bread, driven by a desire for taste. This, of course, has been taken as an opportunity by the supermarkets to produce speciality and organic breads, although they're reticent to discuss the production methods. Those 'in-store bakeries' sometimes just take a chilled loaf and cook it rather than actually make it.

You can buy traditionally produced bread from craft or artisan bakeries, but at a premium price, obviously. I'm afraid cheap prices usually come at the cost of quality, and if you want decent bread you either pay the premium or make your own. Buying in your flour and other ingredients will save you money on buying bread from a shop, about 30 per cent on average. Yes, it will take time but not a lot, and if you batch bake you can freeze bread.

Because you can make whatever size loaf you wish, you can make your loaves to fit your daily needs. If you eat 300g in a day, then make 300g loaves. This alone reduces waste as you don't have loads of stale bread left over. Having said that, you'll find that you eat more bread when you make your own, which is no bad thing. Just as many do on the Continent, replace potatoes with bread in some meals.

There is a drawback to making your own bread. Since it is not full of yummy preservatives, it will go stale more quickly and may grow mouldy faster. (It makes you wonder how good that industrial bread is for you when even mould growth is slowed down.)

Your own bread can be made just as you like. Various types of flour are available, and you can even mix different flours in a bake. You can make all sorts of different shapes, from the traditional tin loaf to rolls, braided breads and baguettes, whatever you fancy.

Your own bread will taste better than anything you can buy from the supermarkets, as the traditional process enables flavour to develop that, in industrial bread, is replaced with extra salt and enhancers. And don't forget that you can't beat the smell of baking bread. The whole house smells wonderful when it's in the oven.

Most importantly, though, your own bread will be better for you.

'Industrial' bread

For hundreds – if not thousands – of years, bread has been made in the same way: flour, salt, fat and water combined with yeast as a raising agent. But in 1961 a new method was developed, known as the Chorleywood process, which reduced both the time needed to make bread and the labour input, thereby reducing manufacturing costs. The age of industrial bread was born.

Traditionally, flour was milled between moving stone wheels – millstones – powered by wind or water, but in the modern age wheat is milled in high-speed steel mills at a high temperature. This smashes apart the starches, making it easier for the enzymes and improvers to work on the flour but reducing the nutritional value. This process also makes the flour able to absorb more water. So when you buy an 800g loaf of industrial bread, you pay for a higher water content. In fact, nearly half of your industrial loaf is water.

This wheat flour is then mixed with water, soya flour, fat, baking aids, ascorbic acid (designated on the packaging as E300) and

yeast. The mixing arms rotate at about 400rpm for around
5 minutes, transferring energy to the dough.

The reaction created by this violent input of energy, assisted by
the ascorbic acid, releases the gluten in the wheat very quickly
and produces a stiff dough in a fraction of the time compared with
the traditional proving process used at home and in craft bakeries.

This part of the process is being linked by some people to an
increase in coeliac disease, a serious gluten intolerance. Although
not proven yet, it is a concern.

An important part of the Chorleywood process is the use of a hard
fat. This works with the gluten to create a stiff dough that will rise
very quickly and retain its structure during the baking and cooling
of the bread. Until recently, hydrogenated fats were used because
these contain more stable heavy fat molecules, which give the fat a
higher melting point.

Recently, bad publicity about hydrogenated fats – in particular
their implication as a key contributor to heart disease – has
created a switch to fractionated fats. These are created from
the processing of ordinary vegetable oils to remove the heaviest
fatty compounds, usually by cooling the oil to make the heavy
fats crystallise. They therefore have the same properties as
hydrogenated fats, and may possibly cause similar health
problems. Often, when manufacturers state that they no longer
use hydrogenated fats, it's likely that they are using fractionated
fats instead.

After mixing, the dough is poured in bulk and left for a few minutes before processing into tins, or onto trays, where it is left to prove for up to an hour (again, perhaps half the time used in traditional bread making).

The Chorleywood bread-making process uses two or three times the usual amount of yeast compared to traditionally made bread. The extra yeast creates a large volume of gas and in the process a spongy loaf. The proving dough may also be put under a low-pressure vacuum to make it rise much faster than if it were at ambient air pressure. This large increase in the amount of yeast we consume in our bread is being cited as one possible cause for the growth of yeast intolerance, irritable bowel syndrome and thrush (candidiasis/*Candida albicans*) disorders over the past few decades.

To help the fats bond to the wet flours, emulsifiers are also added to the mix (usually E471 or E472e). In addition, a small amount of vinegar is added as a preservative. Probably worse than these additives for our health is the addition of relatively large amounts of salt – about double that used in traditional recipes. High salt intake is being linked to heart disease and raised blood pressure.

Finally, your industrial bread with its high water content is an ideal breeding ground for moulds, so it is often dosed with an anti-fungal compound. Yummy!

Primarily because of the milling process, the vitamin content is lower than that of traditional stoneground flour. Accordingly, by law, vitamins are added to the dough mixture to compensate. We take them out, then add them back. Doesn't seem sensible really, does it?

How to bake your own bread

You can buy automatic bread-making machines (see page 109), which have a lot going for them, but you don't need them to make your own bread. People managed perfectly well without them for about 5,000 years.

There are different types of bread: unleavened bread that doesn't use yeast, and breads that use baking powder, sour milk or bicarbonate of soda as raising agents. However, we'll concentrate on 'normal' bread made from wheat flour, just like you buy in the shops (only better). First let's look at the ingredients.

Flour

I strongly recommend you buy organic flour, despite it being at a premium price. Many farmers in the UK and abroad now use a weedkiller called glyphosate on their cereal crops prior to harvesting. The effect on the crop is to kill it off and cause the grain to dry more before harvesting, thereby avoiding the use of dryers to bring the moisture percentage down. This results in glyphosate residues in the grain and resulting flour, which is why glyphosate is now being found in bread. The World Health Organisation has declared glyphosate a possible carcinogen, and some studies indicate it could pose a risk to our kidneys and liver.

Always use a good-quality strong plain flour for bread making, preferably stoneground, which is healthiest. Strong, sometimes called hard, flour is made from wheat with a high gluten content. It's the gluten that enables the bread to stretch and rise. Ordinary flour, like that used for cakes, is not ideal for bread making.

Wholemeal flour contains the whole of the wheat grain, starch, fats and oils, gluten and bran, which provides roughage to help our digestive systems. Lack of roughage has been cited as a cause of bowel cancer, so that's pretty important.

Silly as it may seem, if your wholemeal flour doesn't say 'stoneground' on the pack, then most probably it is reconstituted flour made by taking bleached flour and adding back the bran and wheatgerm which were removed in the industrial milling process.

If wholemeal flour isn't to your taste, you can buy extraction brown flour where some of the bran – between 10 and 20 per cent – has been removed to produce a finer flour. Once again, look for stoneground to get the best nutritional value.

If you'd rather eat white bread (and to be honest, a chip butty just doesn't work with any other bread), then look for unbleached flour. Bleaching does make the bread whiter, but do you really want to eat something that has been bleached? White flour is inferior nutritionally … but one step at a time.

Yeast

Yeast is a microscopic single-celled animal that eats some of the starch and sugars in the flour to produce carbon dioxide. There are about twenty billion cells in a gram of yeast, by the way. Don't worry – they're killed in the baking process! The purpose of yeast in bread is simply to make bubbles of gas that cause the bread to rise and have a lighter texture. Without the action of yeast, your bread would be a solid chewy lump.

You can obtain fresh yeast, but it can be rather difficult to find. Dried yeast is readily available and makes just as good dough. It also stores for much longer and the quantities needed are usually about half those for fresh yeast, making it more economical.

Usually a smaller proportion of yeast is needed for large quantities of flour. Directions for use and quantities are given with each packet. The correct proportions for dried yeast are as follows:

- Up to 700g (1¹/₂ lb) flour – about a teaspoon (5g)
- 700g (1¹/₂ lb) to 1.5kg (3¹/₂ lb flour) – 2tsp (10g)
- 1.5kg (3¹/₂ lb) to 3.2kg (7lb) flour – 3tsp (15g)
- 3.2kg (7lb) to 6.4kg (14lb) flour – 4–5tsp (20–25g)

The yeast needs to be creamed in warm (blood heat) liquid before being added to the flour. Fresh yeast will cream easily in 2 or 3tsp of liquid; dried yeast needs a bit of whisking and more liquid. Fast-acting yeasts do not require any creaming at all – they are simply mixed in with the flour before the liquid is added.

Liquids

Most breads use water, which should be heated to blood heat before it is added to the creamed yeast. For rich mixtures, warmed milk, with or without the addition of a beaten egg, is used. You can also use buttermilk or even whey in place of water. Do not heat the liquid over 110°F/43°C or you will kill off the yeast.

Fats, sugar and salt

Some bread recipes require fats. Butter will give the best flavour for richer yeast mixtures, but margarine may be substituted with good results. Lard may be used for some bread rolls where the characteristic flavour is required. Occasionally you may need to add sugar to some recipes. Most recipes require salt, but you'll be using a tiny amount compared with the salt in commercial bread. For a start, good ingredients have flavour so you don't need huge amounts to fool your taste buds.

Basic method

Having covered the ingredients, let's look at the basic method for making bread. Start with the yeast. Because we're using yeast which must have food, warmth and moisture to grow and produce gas bubbles, we need a nice warm kitchen for best results.

Yeast works best at blood heat (37°C/98.4°F). Too high a temperature will kill the yeast cells, and too low a temperature will slow down the action.

Hopefully your flour is warm. Sieve it with the salt into a large bowl to add air and remove any lumps. If there is any fat being used, rub it in at this stage. Make a well in the centre of the warmed flour and pour in the warmed yeast mixture containing about half the prescribed quantity of milk or water. The liquid is sprinkled with flour, and left to stand for about 20 minutes. This process is known as 'setting the sponge' and improves the bread, although it is not always necessary. The remainder of the liquid is added when the dough is being mixed to its correct consistency.

Mix with a wooden spoon to begin with, and then with your hands until the mixture comes away cleanly from the sides of the bowl. Now comes the fun part where you can relieve your stress by kneading the dough.

The dough must be thoroughly kneaded to develop the elasticity of the gluten. Turn the dough onto a lightly floured surface and knead by lifting and folding one end towards you into the centre, then pushing it down and away from you with the heel of your hand or fist. Turn the dough around a bit and repeat the process. Carry on with this stretching, folding and pushing for about 10 minutes until the dough is firm and elastic and no longer sticks to your hands. Proper kneading is essential to produce the correct texture of baked bread.

If you have an electric mixer, the dough hooks used at a low speed will make short work of kneading the dough, but doing it by hand can be very therapeutic.

After the dough has been thoroughly kneaded, shape it into a ball and put it into a lightly greased bowl. Cover with a slightly damp kitchen towel or with lightly greased cling film to keep it warm and prevent a hard skin from forming. Leave in a warm place for 1–1½ hours to rise, or until it has doubled in size (thanks to the gas from those billions of yeast cells).

The next stage is known as 'knocking back'. Put the risen dough onto your lightly floured board. Knock out the air bubbles with the side of your hand or fist and then knead it again for 2–3 minutes. It should return to its original size and be smooth and firmly elastic again.

You can bake the dough in a suitable loaf tin that fits easily into the oven. Tins should be warmed, well greased and lightly floured. Flat baking trays or round earthenware pots are also used and again need to be warmed and greased before adding the dough.

Next we are going to prove the dough. The dough is divided into suitable portions, shaped and put into the baking tins or onto trays. It is then covered with a clean cloth and put back into a warm place for 30–40 minutes for its final rising until it has again doubled in size. At this stage it is said to be proved.

The bread should be put into the hot oven immediately after the dough has proved. You want the oven to start hot, preheated to kill off the yeast. As a general rule, two tiers of bread may be baked in an oven that has six or more runner positions. Place the upper shelf about halfway down the oven, and the lower shelf on the lowest runner position. When cooking two tiers of bread, heat the oven at Gas Mark 9 (475°F/240°C) for 15 minutes and reduce the oven to Gas Mark 7 (425°F/220°C) when the bread is added to the oven. Interchange loaves on the upper shelf with those on the lower shelf halfway through the baking time.

Small buns or rolls may be baked just above the centre of the oven if one tray is being cooked. If two trays are being baked, arrange one shelf about one-third down the oven and the other shelf about two-thirds down. Bake for the time specified in the recipe; remove the top tray from the oven and move the lower tray to the higher position and continue baking until properly cooked and nicely browned.

Electric fan ovens tend to have an even temperature throughout the oven cavity, which saves the swapping around.

A properly cooked loaf will be well browned all over, have a crisp crust and will sound hollow when tapped on the base. If the base is not quite as crusty as you like, invert the loaf in its tin for a final

5 minutes' baking. As soon as your bread is cooked and removed from the oven, turn out of the tins and leave the loaves on their sides to cool on a wire tray.

There are a lot of different traditional shapes that you can make with your home-made dough. Here are some of the most popular ones. Before you start shaping, divide your dough into the number of pieces you require, cover with a dampened cloth or greased polythene and leave to relax for 5 minutes. This makes the dough easier to shape.

Bloomer loaf

Mould the dough into a fat sausage, and put onto a warmed, greased baking tray. Cover and put to rise. After 25 minutes, make diagonal cuts across the loaf, 6mm ($^1/_4$ in) deep and 3.5cm ($1^1/_2$ in) apart with a sharp knife. Re-cover and put back to rise for a further 15 minutes before baking.

Bread rolls

Divide the dough into 25–40g (1–$1^1/_2$ oz) pieces and form into rolls. Place the rolls on a warmed and greased baking tray, cover and put to rise until they have doubled in size before baking.

Crescents

Roll the dough to a square. Cut in half diagonally to form triangles. Roll each triangle up from the base to the top and draw the ends together to form crescents.

Plaits

Roll out the dough. Cut into 3.5 × 7cm ($1^1/_2$ × 3in) oblongs. Cut each oblong twice through its length to within 2.5cm (1in) of one end. Plait up and seal the loose ends by dampening with water and pressing together.

Twists

Roll out the dough. Cut into 3.5 × 7cm (1$^1/_2$ × 3in) oblongs. Hold one end and twist the dough two or three times.

Vienna rolls

Form into rolls about 7.5cm (3in) long, thicker in the centre than at each end. Make three cuts diagonally across the top with a sharp knife.

Cottage loaf

Cut off one-third of the dough and shape both the large and smaller pieces into smooth balls. Slightly moisten the base of the smaller ball with water and sit it on top of the larger ball and put onto a warmed, greased baking tray. Push the first two fingers of both hands down from the centre of the top ball into the bottom ball to seal the balls together. Cover and put to rise for 40 minutes. If you wish, after 20 minutes, you can make small downward slits with a sharp knife at 5cm (2in) intervals all round the side of the upper and lower parts of the loaf.

Plaited loaf

Divide the dough into either three or five equal pieces and roll each piece into a long sausage. Plait loosely and seal both ends firmly by dampening with water and pressing together. If you're good at plaiting, you can do this with seven equal pieces! Put

onto a warmed, greased baking tray, cover and put to rise for
30–35 minutes before baking.

Split coburg loaf

Mould the dough into a smooth ball, and put onto a warmed and
greased baking tray. Cover and put to rise. After 20 minutes, cut a
cross 1.25cm (½in) deep into the surface of the loaf with a sharp
knife. Put back to rise for another 20 minutes before baking.

Split tin loaf

When the loaf has risen in its tin for about 25 minutes, make a cut
1.25cm (½in) deep from end to end along the centre with a sharp
knife. Re-cover and put the loaf back to rise for a further
15 minutes before baking.

Bread recipes

Wholemeal bread

This is our basic day-to-day bread recipe. It makes four 2lb loaves
or, as we prefer, eight 1lb loves which means one for now and
seven frozen for later. Actually, it's so good fresh, especially with
home-made butter and soup, that we usually only freeze six; the
first two are eaten in a day.

Ingredients

3.2kg (7lb) stoneground wholemeal flour

25g (1oz) salt

4tbsp sunflower oil or 100g (3½oz) lard or white margarine

56g (2oz) fresh yeast or 14g (1oz) dried yeast

2tsp caster sugar

2 litres (3½ pints) water

Method

- Sieve the wholemeal flour into a warm bowl, add the salt and mix well.
- Stir or rub in the oil or fat (depending on what you are using) and leave in a warm place.
- Cream the yeast with the caster sugar and add 900ml (1½ pints) warm water. Leave until frothy.
- Make a well in the centre of the flour and add the yeast mixture.
- Sprinkle with flour and leave for 15–20 minutes to set the sponge.
- Mix to an elastic dough, adding more warm water as necessary.
- Beat well with the hands to mix thoroughly.
- Put into a clean bowl, cover with a damp tea towel and leave to rise in a warm place for about 1 hour, until doubled in size.
- Turn the dough onto a floured board and knead well for 10 minutes.
- Divide the mixture equally into four and knead the pieces again.
- Put into four 900g (2lb) warmed, greased and lightly floured tins, cover with a clean cloth and leave to prove until the dough just reaches the tops of the tins.
- Bake in a preheated oven set at Gas Mark 7 (425°F/220°C) for 45–60 minutes until the loaves sound hollow when tapped at the bottom.
- Cool on a wire rack.

We also make a variant on this recipe, by using stoneground strong white flour and omitting the oil. This results in a lighter but still substantial loaf. Instead of just making eight loaves, we make a couple of loaves and a load of rolls. Wonderful with a home-made pâté.

There's nothing to stop you experimenting a bit with breads. The worst that happens is you don't try that idea again. We've never had to throw an experiment away, or feed it to the hens.

Wholemeal bread is better for you but sometimes it's hard to get children to accept it. Moving from plastic to real bread can be a bit traumatic for them. They're such a conservative bunch with food. Cut the soldiers wrong and the toast is ruined! Try starting with the white flour loaf and then gradually add some wholemeal flour on subsequent bakes. Start with a quarter, next time a half and pretty soon they'll be eating wholemeal bread happily.

Currant bread recipe

You're not limited to just savoury bread – try this one. It's a favourite with children of all ages (including fifty-three!).

Ingredients

675g (1½lb) strong white flour

1tsp salt

50g (2oz) butter or margarine

112g (4oz) currants

14g (½oz) fresh yeast or 7g (¼oz) dried yeast

1tsp caster sugar

400ml (¾ pint) full or semi-skimmed milk

Method

- Mix the flour and salt together in a bowl, rub in the fat, add the currants and leave in a warm place.

- Cream the yeast with the caster sugar and add 150ml (¼ pint) warmed milk. Leave until frothy.

- Make a well in the centre of the flour and add the yeast mixture and enough warmed milk to make a soft dough.

- Turn onto a floured surface and knead for 10 minutes until smooth and elastic.

- Put into a clean bowl, cover with a damp tea towel and leave to rise in a warm place for about 1 hour, until doubled in size.

- Turn onto a floured surface, knock back with your hand or fist to remove any air pockets and then divide into two pieces. Knead each piece again for a few minutes.

- Put into warmed, greased and lightly floured tins, cover with a clean cloth and leave to prove until the dough just reaches the tops of the tins.

- Bake in the centre of a preheated oven set at Gas Mark 6 (400°F/200°C) for about 40 minutes.

- Turn out of the tins and brush immediately with a sugar syrup, which you make by dissolving 50g (2oz) granulated sugar in 60ml (2fl oz) boiling water.

- Leave on a wire tray to cool.

Bread-making machines

I think we all agree that home-made bread is healthier, tastier and generally cheaper than supermarket bread, but it does take time to make. The bread machine is a wonderful compromise. Although they were quite expensive when they came out, now they're quite cheap to buy, often less than £50. Ours cost £10 second-hand, an unused present apparently.

You can enjoy fresh-baked, warm bread in the morning for just 5 minutes' work. Just put the ingredients in the night before, set the timer and take out your loaf in the morning. Two minutes to clean the pan and you're done.

There are some negatives, of course. For a start you can only make one loaf at a time and so your energy cost per loaf can be higher than with batch baking.

Secondly, you are limited to one shape. Having said that, you can use the machine as a mixer to do the hard work of kneading for you and then remove the dough to bake bread rolls and so on in the oven.

Thirdly, some machines don't allow enough time for the yeast to work and the bread can be a little dense.

My advice is that if you are short of time and won't get round to making bread by hand, get a bread maker and a copy of Annette Yates' excellent book *Fresh Bread in the Morning From Your Bread Machine*, which has some excellent recipes.

Tip Don't bother buying those little all-in-one packs to go in the machines. It only takes a moment to measure out the ingredients and it's far cheaper to buy your flour in large bags.

CHAPTER NINE

Making your own butter, cheese and yogurt

Home dairying is becoming quite popular nowadays. Making hard cheese does require specialist equipment, but you can make a passable soft cheese in the kitchen without too much effort. Home-made butter and yogurt are better tasting, very easy to produce and a great way of taking advantage of bargain buys.

Home-made butter is the real thing

If you happen to know a friendly dairy farmer who will let you have cream for a fraction of the shop price, or you find a shop that has over-ordered and is reducing the price of either double or whipping cream, then you can make your own butter for less than you can buy it. Better still, it tastes wonderful, far better than shop-bought. They must add something (I don't know what), but our home-made butter is lighter in colour, spreads more easily and, I suspect, contains a lot less salt.

I don't know how many times I've read that to make butter you put cream into a jar and shake it for hours until it's churned. Well, it does work in the end but I can't really believe that anyone who suggests it does it regularly. Our simple method doesn't give you arm muscles like an Olympic shotputter but does produce wonderful real butter in a short time.

We discovered this when we couldn't resist a shelf of double cream reduced to clear for just 5p. We knew it wouldn't freeze and even our cats couldn't work their way through six tubs, so we decided to make some butter.

The 'ingredients' for butter are simply cream, either whipping or double – single doesn't really work – and possibly a little salt. You can make butter from goat's milk, but it takes a different and far more complex method so let's stick to what we know and can do easily at home.

You do not need much equipment: just a mixing bowl and an electric whisk. I suppose you could try with a hand whisk, but we're back to shotputter's arms then. You can also use a food processor or a Kenwood-type mixer if you are lucky enough to have one.

As long as the cream hasn't turned, it's fine for butter making. In fact, it seems to work more easily if it's on the edge of its date life for some reason. When you get it home it will still be cool from the chiller cabinet. Let the cream reach room temperature, around 20°C (68°F) is ideal – this is critical. Don't heat it but leave the pots out of the fridge for a good few hours to warm up. If you have a cold kitchen, put them into the living room to warm up.

Now we are ready to make butter.

- Proceed as you would for making whipped cream. Use the plastic blades in the processor if you have them. I'm told that the Kenwood 'K' beater is the best tool, but we just use our trusty twenty-year-old electric whisk (that outlasted Yugoslavia where it was made).

- It will go through the usual stage of starting to form firm peaks and then becoming quite stiff. At this point you might like to reduce the speed of your whisk because when it 'goes' it happens very fast. Because it goes so stiff we had problems with the whisk, so we changed from the normal whisk inserts to dough hooks, which coped easily.

- All of a sudden the cream goes a bit yellow in colour and then little bits of butter appear and a thin liquid, the buttermilk. Just seconds later, the butter seems to clump and is separated from the buttermilk. If your whisk is on high speed you'll be redecorating the kitchen by now, hence my suggestion that you reduce speed to a minimum.

- Drain the buttermilk off – you can use this in baking, cooking or even to make your cat very happy. We find it's fantastic in soups. Often we'll make a condensed soup and batch freeze it, adding more water when it's reheated. Adding buttermilk just takes it to a new level, especially with some home-made bread spread with the freshly made butter ... but I digress.

- You need to get all the buttermilk out of the butter or the latter will not store for long and quickly goes rancid. Add clean cold water to the butter in the blender and operate on the lowest speed for a few seconds, or squeeze it by hand in a mixing bowl full of cold water. You need the water to be cold or you melt the butter, which will then run off with the water.

- Squeeze the butter back into a lump, drain off and repeat the washing process until the water is really clean. This can be seven or more times but I can't emphasise enough how you do need to make sure the water is clear. Kneading the butter is a little bit like making bread.

- When you've got the buttermilk out, you need to get the water out of the butter. In the old days special wooden paddles were used to press and shape the butter, but you can use your hands and the back of a spoon. When you have the water out, you are ready for the next stage: salting or flavouring.

Storing butter

Home-made butter can be stored for at least three months in a freezer. I do know that commercial butter stores for much longer but I think they must add stabilisers or something. If you are going to freeze the butter, don't salt or flavour it. The freezing process enhances the saltiness or flavour and you may well find that although it tasted fine when you made it, it is too salty after freezing.

To salt, do not add more than a small $1/2$ tsp for each 250g ($1/2$ lb) of butter – half that amount suits us, but we don't take a lot of salt. You can also add crushed garlic or dried herbs to make flavoured butter at this stage. You'll need to carry out yet more kneading to get it thoroughly mixed in.

Now you can shape the butter and divide it into packs. Butter is best fresh, so we break it into 125g (1/4 lb) portions. Incidentally, even shop-bought butter is best eaten fairly fresh and kept away from direct sunlight. I prefer a roll of butter rather than the traditional box shape. You can then wrap the butter portions in cling film to keep in the fridge or to freeze if you have a lot (but remember not to salt it). I find cling film ideal, but you can use greaseproof paper.

Making butter at home with ordinary kitchen equipment is very easy and a great way to store bargain cream. Like most things made yourself, it tastes exceptional and unique, not to mention the satisfaction of eating something you have made to your personal taste –and saved a little money in the process.

Make cheese in your kitchen

A lot of people are put off the idea of making cheese at home because of having to buy special equipment and supplies, but cottage or curd cheese is really easy to make and requires no more tools than you would find in an ordinary kitchen. It also does not need rennet or any special ingredients.

Making cheese has always been a way of storing a surplus of milk for use when the cow or sheep was dry, and it's a great way to store any surplus milk you may find yourself with at home. In terms of cost, home-made cheese will not save you money if you make it from full-priced milk, but if you have a couple of pints about to turn in the fridge or the supermarket has overstocked and reduced some milk, you can store this by making cottage cheese. **Although cottage cheese – or curd cheese as some people call it – doesn't store for a long time in the fridge, it will freeze easily.**

We've never found out how long our cottage cheese will keep because it tends to be eaten quickly. This method produces a different cheese from commercial cottage cheese. It's firmer and more granular, which we like, and you can add different flavourings, but we just like salt and black pepper.

All cheeses are made from the coagulated lumps from milk – the curds – with the liquid part called the whey (hence 'curds and whey'). Although a lactic starter can be used when making cottage cheese, it is not necessary. The same chemical reaction of turning the milk, or curdling, can be obtained by the use of vinegar or lemon juice, which most people already have in their kitchen.

So why not spend half an hour making your own cottage cheese? It tastes better than shop-bought and the process is absolutely fascinating. You don't need any special equipment, just a saucepan, wooden spoon and a fine sieve.

The method is pretty straightforward as well:

- Pour the milk into a saucepan and heat it on the hob until it is very hot, but not boiling. You must not boil it. Stir occasionally with the wooden spoon.
- Take it off the heat and allow it to cool for a couple of minutes, then add lemon juice or vinegar (1 × 15ml tbsp per 570ml/

1 pint milk). That's about right but we're not scientists; a little more or less won't make much difference.

- Stir gently, and magically the milk will split into the curds and whey. Let it cool down and pour through your fine sieve to catch the curds. You can discard the whey butter but it's far better to use it instead of water in bread making, or in any recipe calling for sour milk or buttermilk.
- Transfer the curds to a bowl and add a pinch of salt. (Another benefit of making your own is that you are in control of the salt content. The amount of salt added to most foods we buy is horrendous.)
- Now you can add extra flavourings, if you wish. We like a sprinkle of black pepper but you can add chopped chives or spring onions, herbs or whatever takes your fancy. If you want it really rich and creamy, add a tablespoon of double cream. Sheer luxury!

If your milk doesn't curdle, it may be the milk you are using. For this cheese, use only regular pasteurised milk, **not UHT**. Try adding a little more acid in the form of lemon juice or vinegar to correct the balance if it's not the milk that's causing the problem.

Having made your own cottage cheese, you might fancy trying something a little more ambitious. It's quite possible to make all sorts of cheese at home: hard cheeses like Cheddar or soft ones like Brie. You'll need more in the way of equipment and you'll need to research the subject in more depth. Don't forget you'll need a low-cost source of milk to produce anything at less cost than you can buy in the shops.

Yogurt – easier than you may think

It always amazes me to see shelves of different yogurts in the supermarket. It is one of the easiest dairy products to make at home. You don't need any special equipment (although a yogurt maker will make life easier if you start making it in volume).

The raw material for yogurt is quite simply milk. You can use semi-skimmed or full-fat pasteurised milk, but the process is a little easier using UHT or sterilised milk. UHT is generally the cheapest milk to buy. You can also make yogurt from goat's milk or sheep's milk. Different milks will change the yogurt. Semi-skimmed milk will produce a thinner consistency, but you can add milk powder to semi-skimmed to thicken it up or even use cream.

The only other material you need is a bacterial starter. The easiest way to obtain this is to buy a small pot of live yogurt. Just look for the word 'live' on the tub. Usually natural or probiotic yogurts will be live (check the small print on the side). Most flavoured yogurts are not live (they've been heat treated to increase shelf life, killing off the bacteria), but live yogurt isn't hard to find, even in the supermarket.

Some health food shops will sell specific yogurt starters but you really don't need to go to that expense. Different starters will make a difference to the final product. Experimenting is half the fun.

You don't need to buy a fresh starter every time you make a batch of yogurt; just hold back a little from your last. After a number of times around, the starter can lose its strength. If that happens, just buy another pot of live yogurt, which is an opportunity to try a different starter.

Apart from ordinary kitchen equipment, all you need is a thermometer that can be dipped into liquid and a wide-necked thermos flask. You can buy special yogurt makers. We got ours for a pound at a car-boot sale, and they do make things a little easier as temperature is finely controlled. Incidentally, they only use minimal amounts of electricity, no more than 15 watts.

To make your first batch of yogurt you'll need:

570ml (1 pint) milk

2tbsp 'live' yogurt

- If you are using pasteurised milk, you need to sterilise it. Put the milk into a pan and bring to the boil, hold there for 1 minute (being careful it doesn't boil over – stirring helps), and then remove from the heat.
- Allow the milk to cool to 37°C (98.4°F) (just about body temperature). A thermometer is useful here. If you're using UHT or sterilised milk, just heat the milk to body heat.
- Take a pre-warmed mixing bowl or a large jug and put in 2tbsp live yogurt, then add a little of the warm milk. Mix well until smooth and then add the rest of the milk, stirring thoroughly.
- If you're making your yogurt in a thermos flask, warm the inside with hot water first before pouring in the yogurt base. Put the lid on and leave for 7–8 hours until it has turned into yogurt and set.

You can try other ways to keep the temperature correct – a pan in an airing cupboard or a very low oven – but you do need to make certain that the temperature remains fairly constant. If it gets too hot, the mixture curdles; if too cool it won't set. A proper yogurt maker is far easier than other methods, apart from a thermos, at keeping the temperature constant. It should have instructions specific to the machine.

Once made, keep your yogurt in the fridge; it should keep for 4 or 5 days. It is ideal for cooking or eating as plain yogurt, but you can add flavourings if you wish at this stage. Leave it in the fridge for a few hours to cool and further thicken before adding your flavours. Mashed banana, strawberries or peaches go well.

It really is that easy to make your own, but you can also take things one step further and make a soft cheese from your yogurt. You'll need some cheesecloth or muslin for this.

- Line a colander with the cloth and pour the freshly made yogurt into it, then allow it to drain for an hour or so.
- Take the cloth by the corners and lift it out, tie tightly and hang off the kitchen tap to allow it to drain further. Usually another hour is sufficient; by this time no more liquid will be dripping out.
- Add a little salt and pepper to taste; perhaps some chopped chives will make an interesting soft cheese for you. It should keep for about the same time as your yogurt.

CHAPTER TEN

Making your own wine, beer and cider

It can't have escaped your notice that every year the government happily increases the tax rate on alcohol. For those of us who enjoy a glass of wine with a meal, or the odd beer, it's bad news. Of course, they cite health reasons and an aim to reduce binge drinking, but they punish us responsible drinkers along with the minority.

If you buy a very modest bottle of still wine for £5, the tax element of the price (in 2017) will be over £3. Add in the shipping, packaging and profit for the retailer and the actual amount the producer gets is a tiny 45p!

Therefore, if we want to enjoy a little luxury but don't want to pay through the nose, we can make our own (and watch the taxman weep).

The benefits of home winemaking

Although you can save money making your own wine, there's little point if the wine you make is awful and nobody wants to drink it. I'd suggest the best way to get started is by making your wine from grape concentrate or kits. Like any craft, it takes a while to acquire the necessary skills and starting this way means you are far more likely than not to get at least an acceptable result.

Once you've got to grips with the processes (and worked out what went wrong on the odd disaster) you can move on to more advanced 'country' wines from fruits and even vegetables that you will enjoy.

Having said that, I don't want you to think it's rocket science. People have been making wine for thousands of years using the most basic equipment and today we have far superior tools to do the job, which makes life a lot easier.

Equipment

You will need to get some equipment – don't forget to check out the second-hand market first – but it's not too expensive to get started. You can buy starter kits for as little as £25 that will provide all you need apart from things that you will have in the kitchen anyway. Do check exactly what is included and compare with buying the parts separately. I'd suggest buying separately as you'll be making larger quantities as time goes on; this is an addictive hobby.

You'll need:

- **Large saucepan** If you have a preserving pan for jam making, that will be fine.

- **Demijohns** We use 1-gallon large glass bottles, fitted with a bored rubber bung into which the airlock fits. Nowadays you can buy 5-litre plastic versions already fitted with a grommet for the fermentation airlock. The airlock allows excess carbon dioxide produced by the yeast to escape but stops air loaded with wild yeasts and so on getting back in.

- **Kitchen thermometer** Temperature control is important in wine making.

- **Measuring jug and kitchen scales** Which you should have anyway.

- **Large food grade plastic bin with lid** For when you start making country wines.

- **Plastic siphoning tube** Usually you can buy this by the metre. A couple of metres should not set you back more than a pound.

- **Hydrometer** This is a device used to measure the sugar content. Technically, it compares the weight of the liquid to that of water. You can buy high-tech digital versions or a manual type for a couple of pounds that will last for decades.

- **Bottles, labels, corks and seals** A corking machine is pretty useful, especially if you're making a fair quantity. Just save some wine bottles, obviously. The labels can be fancy or cheap depending on how you feel, but you do need to label your wine or you'll forget what's in the bottle. Corks can be bought for just a few pence each in bags of 100. Never reuse corks. No matter how you try to sterilise them, used corks will spoil your wine. Corking machines can be bought from just a couple of pounds up to £60. We found the twin-lever type for around £10 far better than the cheapest ones.

Making your wine

Before you start making your wine, it's worth looking at the process that converts fruit juice to wine. It's quite simply yeasts converting sugars to alcohol and carbon dioxide. Yeasts are tiny organisms just floating around in the air – leave a cup of grape juice on the side and within hours there will be some some yeasts in there.

Unfortunately there are many types of yeast, and wild yeasts are more likely to produce vinegar than wine. That's why you buy your yeast for wine making. Wine yeasts have been developed over the years to withstand a high level of alcohol, and you can just buy an all-purpose wine yeast. When you begin to get more confident and develop the art, you can move on to specialised varieties: Burgundy, Chablis, Hock, Sauterne and Champagne yeasts, to name but a few. Don't be tempted to use bread yeast. Trust me; it doesn't work well for wine!

Because of the wild yeasts in the air, it is critical that you maintain the highest standards of cleanliness and sterilise your equipment. You cannot skimp on this or you'll end up with a lot of vinegar at best.

Once your army of tiny yeasts has finished working, you have wine but it's not really drinkable. Time is a great healer, so they say, and it certainly changes harsh undrinkable rotgut into sublime wine. Once bottled, you lay down your wine for anything from a few months to a few years. This is an area where the art comes into play. We've opened a bottle only to pour it down the sink. One year

later we tried the same wine again and ended up drinking
two bottles in one evening.

Before you start, sterilise the equipment you are about to use, even
if it appears perfectly clean. You could use lots of boiling water
and bicarb, but it is a lot easier and more reliable to buy some
specific sterilising chemical. There are a few on the market, but
we found that even the ones that claim not to need rinsing actually
do. You can also use Campden tablets for sterilising, but the
specifically designed products are better at cleaning.

If you didn't clean your equipment thoroughly after the last time
you used it, you may need to leave things to soak for an hour or
three. A bottle brush, especially the long-handled type that can get
into the corners of a demijohn, is very useful here.

The general method for most wine made from concentrates is
to combine the concentrate with hot water and sugar, mixing
thoroughly to dissolve the sugar. You may have to add some citric
acid as well for best results. Usually the concentrate pack will give
you the specific recipe details. Often you only add part of the sugar
initially, adding the rest as a syrup after the initial fermentation
has slowed down.

Then allow your base – it's called a 'must' – to cool to below blood
heat (37°C/98.4°F) before adding your yeast or you'll kill it. You
can also add yeast nutrient, which is really like a booster for the
yeast. We found it really helpful.

Pour into the demijohns, leaving some headroom or it will bubble up into the airlock and could breach the seal. Fix the bung and airlock on. Don't forget you need to add sterile (boiled from the kettle is fine) water in the airlock. That's what seals it against wild yeast getting in.

Now put your demijohn somewhere warm. Ideally, you want to maintain it at about 18–20°C (64–68°F) so an airing cupboard is ideal, although with good insulation on the tank they're not as warm as they used to be. You can buy little electric blankets for demijohns, but that's an additional cost.

After a few hours you'll see little bubbles of air coming through the airlock and these will speed up quite quickly. A little foam will appear on the surface and the plop of bubbles coming through the airlock will get faster and faster. Sometimes it can take a day before the fermentation takes off. If it's much longer, assume that something has gone wrong with the yeast. You can usually rescue the situation by adding 1tsp yeast to a cup of sugar solution and adding that once it's bubbling.

After the initial rush, things slow down and this is where you add extra syrup if the recipe calls for it. Once again, things speed up and then calm again. Now you just need to be patient and leave things alone for about six weeks until the airlock is hardly bubbling or stopped. Now we move onto the next stage: racking.

Racking and bottling

Down at the bottom of your demijohn there will be a layer of yeast and sediment. We don't want this in the wine: it doesn't taste good and it spoils the look.

Sterilise another demijohn and some plastic siphoning tube, then carefully siphon off the wine from the first demijohn into the new one. To do this, put the full demijohn onto an upturned bucket or similar so that its base is above the top of the empty demijohn. Insert your tube just an inch or two and then suck on the other end to fill the tube with wine. Once filled, place the end of the tube into the top of the lower, clean demijohn and the wine will start to flow from one to the other.

You need to use a little skill and judgement now. The idea is to get the wine and leave the sludge behind. Be very gentle and, as the end of the siphon gets near the bottom, keep your eye on the tube as well. If it suddenly sucks up the gunk, pinch the tube off or close it with your thumb.

Now we want to stop any further action by the yeast organisms by killing them off. Add one Campden tablet crushed and mixed with boiled water. Campden tablets are made of sodium metabisulphite and they release sulphur dioxide, a powerful sterilising agent.

Top up your wine to just under the neck of the demijohn with cooled boiled water and put a solid bung into the jar. Leave it in a cool, dark place and sediments will continue to settle out. After three months it should be bright and clear, ready to bottle.

You can hasten this clearing process by adding wine finings as you rack. These will cause the remaining sediments to clear in a day or two but since all home-made wine improves with age, usually just leave it to time.

Now you can rack the wine again or bottle it. With a kit wine, I'd just bottle and I'd probably have used the finings to hurry things along. Don't forget it's critical to have clean, sterile bottles. If there is old sediment in a bottle, don't use it.

You need to soften natural corks in boiling water, which sterilises them, and then cork the bottles. You can get plastic wrappers that you place over the cork end of the bottle and shrink-wrap them on with a hairdryer. They look most professional.

Label with the name and, most importantly, the date, place in a wine rack and test your strength of character. The longer you leave it, the better the wine.

Country wines

Once you have developed some confidence, you can move on to making country wines. I can see French wine purists burning this book in horror, but we have a wonderful tradition of making wines in the UK from the most unlikely ingredients.

I once happened on a bargain buy of canned orange pulp. It made a fabulous wine and I must admit – when we had a party – one racked demijohn never even made it to the bottle. From siphon to glass, but sadly I don't recall all the details of that party!

With most country wines, the main difference from grape wines is that we provide extra sugar primarily to feed the yeast. When we needed to crush fruits like blackberries, we found the easiest way was to use an old-fashioned potato masher. Here's a recipe for a gallon of blackberry wine that was really nice after just a year in the bottle (and was fabulous after two).

Blackberry wine

Ingredients

1.5kg (3lb) or so good ripe blackberries

same weight sugar

cooled boiled water

2 Campden tablets

1tsp Pectolase pectin enzyme

yeast, small single sachet

yeast nutrient tablet

Method

- Crush the blackberries in a large bowl or saucepan with a potato masher or whatever comes to hand. Pour over 1.1 litre (2 pints) of cooled boiled water to which you have added the Campden tablets and the Pectolase. (The Campden tablets will kill off the wild yeasts on the fruit. The Pectolase is a pectin-destroying enzyme. If you don't use it, the wine will develop a pectin haze, which spoils the appearance.)
- Cover and leave for a day.
- Make up a syrup by dissolving 400g sugar in 1 litre water (1lb to 2 pints) and pour this into a sterilised, large food-grade plastic bucket with a lid. Then strain the blackberry juice through a fine sieve into the syrup and add the crushed yeast nutrient tablet and all-purpose wine yeast.
- Keep the bucket in a warm place for a week, giving it a stir every day. Pour into a demijohn, leaving as much sediment behind as you reasonably can. We strained through a jelly bag,

but in hindsight this isn't necessary as you'll be racking off later anyway.

- Make up the rest of the sugar into a syrup and add to the demijohn, and then make it up using cooled boiled water. Don't pour hot syrup in; you will kill the yeasts. Fit the bung and airlock and leave for six weeks or so to ferment. Keep the demijohn in the dark as light will spoil the colour of the wine.

- Once fermentation has stopped, or slowed to just the odd bubble, rack off into a sterilised demijohn and top up to the neck with cooled boiled water to which you have added a Campden tablet to stop the yeast from continuing to ferment.

- Rack again after three months, adding finings if the wine is hazy, and allow to settle for a few days before bottling up. Now this is where you need to be self-controlled. Forget it is there until you go blackberrying again next year when you may try a bottle.

Home brewing

Unlike wines, in beers the yeast is converting starches to alcohol and we're not leaving the beer to mature for a year or two before drinking. The alcohol strength of our beer will be far less than that of wine, but be careful: home-made beers are often stronger than you expect.

Once again, it's easiest to start with a kit beer. There's a huge range of concentrates available, formulated for different flavours and styles from lagers to dark bitter beers. Concentrates generally work out a little dearer than making your beer from scratch, which requires you obtaining hops, malt extract, malted grains, etc.

Unlike wines, you can make beers in a plastic bin without the airlocks and so on, or in a fermenter. Beers are ready to bottle in a matter of ten days or so, but rather than individually bottling (which requires beer bottles, caps and a machine to apply them) most people nowadays use purpose-made tapped barrels and just pour out as required.

From a financial viewpoint, making your own beer will save you money on shop-bought beer. You can end up with a decent beer from just 50p a pint.

Usually the kit beers just comprise a tin with the base malt, etc, and a packet of yeast. You warm the opened tin to soften the contents and mix with boiling water and sugar. A kilogram pack of sugar is usual and will result in a beer with a strength of around 5.2 per cent. You then put this into your fermenting bin and top up with cold water to 5 gallons. Most kits are geared for 40 pints (5 gallons).

When the liquor has reached room temperature, add the yeast and that's about it until you bottle up or put into a barrel. A couple of weeks later you will be drinking your own beer.

Once you have mastered kit beers, you can move on to buying the base ingredients and making beers from scratch.

Cider

If you happen on a source of apples, then cider is a great way to use up a glut. Some 'experts' say to use only cider apples, others mainly dessert and others mainly cooking, but in reality most home cider makers use whatever apples that they have at hand; even a proportion of crab apples is fine.

They don't even need to be in perfect condition; bruised and slightly damaged apples are fine for this. If the apples have fallen from the tree, don't be afraid to use them too, unless they've started to rot. Do watch out for wasps when picking up apples. If I had a pound for every time I've been stung. I'd be writing this in Barbados.

You want to keep your apples somewhere cool for a week or two to soften the skins if they're hard. Before processing, wash the apples to remove any soil or insects.

The hardest part of making cider is getting the juice out. With small quantities you can try cutting them up and putting them through a food processor or a juicer, but it's really not worth the effort.

To get any decent amount of juice, you need a fruit press and crusher. If you can't justify a crusher, then you can get a cheap device called a Pulpmaster which attaches to an electric drill. It is just a blade that cuts the apples up and you can buy it with a bin. The shaft goes through the bin lid, which stops the contents splashing everywhere, or you can construct your own using an old fermenting bin and drilling the hole for the shaft through it, so that all you need to buy is the blade attachment.

Presses can be bought from just £50 to the frankly ridiculous. Try for a good second-hand one.

Traditional scrumpy cider would rely on the natural yeasts on the apples for the fermentation process, but that's very hit and miss.. The best way is to add one Campden tablet per gallon to kill off the wild yeasts and then add a proper wine yeast a few hours later. A Champagne yeast is ideal, but a general wine yeast will suffice. You don't need to add any yeast nutrient as a rule, but it can do no harm. Ferment in a large beer fermenter.

Since your apples will vary, so will the sugar content of the juice. If there is too little sugar, then the cider may not have enough alcohol to keep well. You can find this out with your hydrometer. If the specific gravity is 1070 or over, then you are OK but, if it is below this, add some sugar syrup to get it up to 1070.

When the cider has finished fermenting, check the specific gravity which should now be around 1005. Rack it off to get rid of the sediments and leave for a couple of days to settle further. If need be, rack it off again using finings if it won't clear and you're bothered about the appearance.

Now you can add one Campden tablet per gallon to stop fermentation before bottling. You can use plastic fizzy drink bottles for cider, or glass if you prefer. Cider has a nasty habit of restarting fermentation, so be careful with glass bottles as they can explode. Loosen the tops occasionally to release any pressure build-ups. Alternatively, keep in the beer fermenter and have a party.

Don't forget that you can also make perry – pear cider – in exactly the same way. However, do use some yeast nutrient with perry; it seems to need it.

CHAPTER ELEVEN

Food for free

It's got to be appealing – the chance to get something for nothing just makes any 'frugal-living' person sit up and take note.

As we saw in Chapter 2, the huge amount of food just chucked away by supermarkets and sandwich bars is appalling. A lot of this waste is food that's not sold before its sell-by date. Usually it's perfectly safe but the supermarket dare not risk someone suing them if it was off. Sometimes it's just not fresh; a sandwich shop selling slightly stale bread is not long for the business world.

Not so long ago, this food waste – along with that from school meals and hospital kitchens –would have been used to feed pigs, but this is illegal since the 2001 foot-and-mouth outbreak that was traced to illegally imported meat.

Some supermarkets have a wonderful approach to food which, at the end of its sell-by date, hasn't sold when reduced. They leave it outside the store, free to take away. Some give it to charity, but most just dump it in bins at the back. You may have heard of the

Freegans who advocate reclaiming this food from the bins. Sadly this is illegal. Technically it is theft – and probably trespass – so I can't really advocate this. It's just a shame that the shops don't all make it available to those who want and need it.

If you still have a greengrocer in your area – sadly a very endangered species – it's worth asking if he has any green waste, such as leaves cut from cauliflowers, etc. They may not be ideal for you, but they're great for feeding chickens.

It's amazing how many gardens, and even some verges, boast apple trees, but the apples are just left to fall on the ground and rot. At worst they can be converted into cider. I noticed a neighbour was often away and asked her about the fruit on her trees. She was happy to see it being used rather than become a rotting mess on the grass, which needed cleaning up when she returned home.

Do be thoughtful with trees by the roadside. They may technically be on public land and the fruit therefore free to all, but sometimes people living nearby get very possessive. If challenged, be diplomatic even if you're in the right.

The roadside verge is also a source of those most traditional of free foods: the blackberries, elderflowers and berries. There is far more available, but you'll need to get out of the car and walk down those country lanes to find it. The blackberry patch you spot as you race by at 40mph has already been spotted and stripped by another driver anyway.

Foraging for hedgerow foods is a great family day out. Take a picnic and give the children enjoyment not just on that particular day but also when they eat the fruits of their labours.

While there is a huge range of edible wild plants available in the UK, edible is not the same as appetising. Many are the wild versions of our present-day vegetables that have been selected for yield and flavour over hundreds of generations. I've listed below those we think worth foraging for.

Before you start harvesting your wild free foods, there are a few things to remember:

- Don't strip the whole plant or dig it up. Leave something for the wildlife.
- Avoid hedgerows by roads with high traffic volumes. Although we now use lead-free petrol, there will be diesel soot and other pollutants.
- Avoid picking from hedgerows that have been recently sprayed with herbicides and pesticides. Although this can be hard to spot, look for lots of browning and dying weeds.

Fruits for free

Bilberries

These are most often found in wet acid soils; boggy areas are worth checking out. Lovely when cooked, but far too tart when raw.

Blackberries

The commonest and most prolific wild berry. Those that survive being eaten when picked make wonderful jam, or a jelly if the pips bother you. Don't forget blackberry and apple pie! If you come across a lot and can't use them immediately, drop them into a pan of water, which will cause any little bugs to float off, and then freeze to use later in pies or jams.

Crab apples

Crab apple jelly. Need I say more? Keep an eye out for crab apple trees in suburban gardens as well. Often the fruit is a nuisance to the owner who may be happy to give it away.

Elderberries

As a child I was told that elderberries were poisonous, which tends to put you off. In fact unripe elderberries do contain tiny traces of cyanide and could cause vomiting and diarrhoea. So only pick ripe elderberries, which are plump and dark black in colour. Just take them in bunches. You can strip the berries off the twigs at home.

Elderberries are best eaten cooked anyway, which makes them safe if a few unripe berries have missed your eye. They aren't the best-flavoured berry, although they are good for you, so we tend to use them with other fruits in jams. Blackberry and elderberry works well, but you can make an elderberry jelly. Very traditional country cottage fare.

Elderflower

Yes, you can eat them. Some people swear that they like elderflower fritters, but for me the best use is in elderflower champagne. If you're teetotal, then you can make an elderflower cordial that's non-alcoholic. Here's a recipe:

Elderflower cordial

Ingredients

1kg (2.2lb) bag ordinary white sugar

850ml (1½ pints) boiling water

20 or so elderflower heads, shaken to remove any wildlife (don't wash the flavour away)

1 or 2 unwaxed lemons, grated and cut into slices

25g citric acid (available from chemists or some supermarkets)

Method

- Put the sugar into a large mixing bowl and pour on the boiling water, stirring to dissolve. Add all the other ingredients, stirring to mix well.
- Leave for 24 hours in a cool place, covered with a tea towel to allow the flavours to infuse.
- Pour into clean screw-top bottles and chill to serve.

It keeps quite well – I've been told a couple of months – but has never lasted more than a week in our house!

Hawthorn

I'm told the young leaves are edible, but I think you need to be starving to really appreciate them. The berries work well with crab apples in a jelly, though, so it's worth harvesting a few. Don't be greedy with them. They're important to wild birds as a food source.

Raspberries

You'll often find self-seeded raspberries happily growing in the wild. Usually these are just domestic ones who've been 'sown' by a bird for you. Being free, they do taste better than those grown in captivity.

Rosehips

You can buy rose cultivars especially bred for the hips, but wild rosehips are fine. They're rarely seen in manicured gardens where the flowers are deadheaded, so the rosehip fruit never gets a chance to develop. Once again, don't be greedy, as they're an important food supply for wild birds, being ready for picking in October as winter approaches fast.

Their main use is in rosehip syrup, which came into vogue in Britain during World War II when it was realised that we had an abundant source of vitamin C just growing wild. Rosehips contain twenty times the vitamin C of fresh oranges. They also make a nice wine.

The classic recipe for rosehip syrup comes from the Ministry of Food publication *The Hedgerow Harvest,* published in 1943, for 900g (2lb) hips:

- Boil 1.7 litres (3 pints) water.
- Mince the hips in a coarse mincer (we use a food processor nowadays or a juicer) and put immediately into the boiling water.
- Bring back to the boil and then place aside for 15 minutes.
- Pour into a nylon or cotton jelly bag and allow to drip until the bulk of the liquid has come through.
- Return the residue to the saucepan, add 850ml (1½ pints) boiling water, stir and allow to stand for 10 minutes.

- Pour back into the jelly bag and allow to drip.
- To make sure all the sharp hairs are removed, put back the first half cupful of liquid and allow to drip through again.
- Put the mixed juice into a clean saucepan and boil down until the juice measures about 850ml (1^1/$_2$ pints), then add 560g (1^1/$_4$ lb) of sugar and boil for a further 5 minutes.
- Pour into hot sterile bottles and seal at once. Store in a dark place.

It's best to use small bottles or jars as the syrup will only keep for a week after opening. Once opened, keep in the fridge.

Rowanberries

The mountain ash or rowan tree is most often found in the north and west of the country. The berries look a little like elderberries except they're bright orange. Harvest like elderberries to make a jelly, usually with crab apples which supply the additional pectin needed for a set.

Sloes

The fruit of the blackthorn can be found almost anywhere in the British Isles and is the basis of that country favourite, sloe gin. My Norwegian friend told me that they use sloes in his country but for making aquavit rather than gin. I think the implication was that real men drank aquavit. Since I like neither, we have sloe brandy.

It's best to wear gloves when harvesting, by the way. Sloes have quite wicked spikes.

- Take 450g (1lb) or so of sloes after the first frosts of the year in October. If there hasn't been a frost you'll need to prick the skins with a darning needle.
- Put into a sterilised jar – we use a Kilner-style jar – along with 250g (9oz) granulated white sugar and a litre of brandy.
- Seal the jar and give a good shake, then put in a cool, dark place. Give it another good shake every day for a week and then once a week until Christmas when it will be ready.

You can strain the liquid and serve the sloes as a dessert (adults only) with whipped cream, drinking the liqueur after the meal as I vaguely recall.

Nuts for nothing

Hazelnuts

They're quite common across most of the country, but they don't really like a wet soil so don't bother hunting in boggy ground. By mid-September to October the leaves begin to turn colour and the hazelnuts are ready. The trick is to beat the squirrels to it. Check under the bush for dropped nuts as well.

Sweet chestnuts

Often you'll find these in public parks. They are easily identified by the husks, which are incredibly prickly, unlike conkers. You need thick gloves and good boots; the prickles will go straight through the sole of trainers. Roasted chestnuts, especially on an open bonfire, just make winter special.

Walnuts

Just occasionally you may be lucky and come across a walnut tree, planted many years ago and now forgotten. Keep the secret as well as the bounty.

Herbs and greenery

As I said earlier, many of our vegetables' ancestors are growing wild and are edible if not appetizing. The following stand out as worth looking for:

Horseradish

You can grow horseradish in the garden but it takes a fair bit of room. If you spot one wild and available, then head back with a spade in midsummer. Don't take the whole root, just some pieces. The plant will continue to grow for years to come. You can make a base for horseradish sauce that will store well.

Long-keeping horseradish sauce

- Make up a syrup of equal volumes of white vinegar and granulated white sugar – about 300ml (1/2 pint) of each is fine – with 1tsp salt. Dissolve the sugar on a low heat and allow to cool.
- Wash well and peel the root under water. You know how onions can make you cry? Well, horseradish is more like CS gas! Cut roughly and put into a food processor or through a fine mincer. If you have some of those DIY safety goggles you can buy cheaply, it is worth putting them on when processing horseradish.
- Take a sterilised Kilner-type jar and put in a little of the minced horseradish, then pour on some syrup. When it has

settled, add more horseradish and then more syrup, repeating until the jar is full. It should keep for a year like this in a cool, dark place.

When you want some horseradish sauce to accompany Sunday lunch or to perk up a cold beef sandwich, just take out a tablespoonful and mix with double cream and a little extra wine vinegar and a teaspoon of mustard if you wish. If you have no cream you can use crème fraîche or even a white sauce, although the latter doesn't really work so well.

Mushrooms

Wild mushrooms are delicious but there's one major problem: some mushrooms are poisonous. In rural French villages they have a rather clever system where you pick your mushrooms and drop into the local pharmacy with them. They check them over and confirm you've not got any poisonous ones in the basket.

A good book with full colour photographs can help, but for safety you really need to go mushroom hunting with someone who knows what they are doing. Once you know what you're looking at, you can be sure you're cooking a meal rather than a last meal.

Nettles

Usually used in a soup, nettles are a good source of vitamins and antioxidants. Wear gloves to pick the young nettle tips unless you have a pain threshold that would qualify you for the SAS. I can't honestly say I'm a fan of nettle soup, but tastes differ.

Seaweeds

If you live near the sea you can collect seaweed. If there's masses on the beach, then bag it up for the garden. The small amount of salt won't do any harm and the nutrients will boost your crops.

Late spring and early summer are the best times to find seaweeds. If the strands are loose, perhaps washed up in a storm, then take the lot; if they're anchored cut no more than half the length of the strand so there's enough left to regrow.

Perhaps the best-known edible seaweed in Britain is laver, which is used to make the famous Welsh laverbread.

Wild garlic

Your nose will guide you to this herb. Much milder than the cultivated garlic, it's the leaves you're after here. It's rather nice added to a salad or mixed with mayonnaise as a dressing.

CHAPTER TWELVE

Grow your own

There's no doubt that all of us would prefer to eat organic wholesome food, given the choice. After all, who wants to eat pesticide residues, the effects of which may not come to light for years? Despite assurances that such residues in food are safe, the truth is that only a minute percentage of products are tested and a worrying number of those fail, containing more residues than allowed by law.

Worse still is something called the 'cocktail effect'. We may know with some confidence what a safe level is for pesticide A and the same for pesticide B, but what is the safe level when mixed? There are too many permutations to check, so we just guess and hope that they're safe in combination. I don't want to be a scaremonger, but it does suggest that organic foods are safer.

Sadly, not all organic foods may actually be so. Economic pressures can lead suppliers to cheat, and a number of cases of organic eggs that weren't actually organic have been found. Growing your own means you are in total control of the inputs and usually you can get away without any pesticides, or a least minimal use of which you are aware.

Ecologically, growing your own means a huge reduction in carbon emissions. Those food miles just don't apply when the only travel is from garden to kitchen by foot. The economics are encouraging as well. Ordinary food is fairly expensive, and organic food is only really affordable for the well off. That's not because the farmers or supermarkets are making huge profits, by the way. The reason is that growing food organically is more labour-intensive and not as productive per acre, so it inevitably costs more.

In one year the average family could save anything from £800 upwards by growing their own; more if you compare the savings against organic fruit and vegetables. Of course, you have to work for that saving – vegetables don't grow without some assistance – but it's more fun than work, keeps you fit and is immensely satisfying.

How much land . . . and how to find it

To supply fully all the fruit and vegetables required by a family of four, you need about 250 square metres (300 square yards) of land, so the first problem for most of us in modern houses with postage-stamp-sized gardens is where to find it.

The first choice would have to be the traditional allotment. Unfortunately, there is a national shortage with an estimated 100,000 people on allotment waiting lists. Still, many areas have vacancies and even those with waiting lists may have a vacancy come up fairly quickly. A lot of people get on more than one waiting list too, so that can distort the figures.

If you don't know where your local allotments are, ask at the library and the council. Then make yourself known on the site. It's surprising how it can help you to move up the list when the site manager knows who you are and that you are really keen.

Another option is to look around for overgrown gardens. There are many elderly people, no longer as physically active as they once were, who would be happy to see their garden become productive again, especially if you share the produce with them – not to mention giving them some company to chat to.

It's not just the elderly, though. The 'city busy' may like the idea of a garden but not have the time to look after it. Instead of paying a gardener – another example of the madness of working all hours to pay someone to undertake jobs that are actually a pleasure – they may well be happy to allow you to garden for them. They get a tidy garden, you get the produce.

Perhaps you have some wasteland near, just growing weeds. If it is owned by the council and you get together with a few other people and make an approach, then there's a chance they may let you work the land. Even commercial owners may prefer to see the land in use than costing money to maintain.

Even the postage-stamp garden can be productive, though, so don't write it off. Of course, a garden has to do more than grow some vegetables and house some chickens. The children need somewhere to play, you need somewhere to barbecue or just sit, and it needs to be attractive. But those other demands don't stop you making it productive as well.

Don't forget the front garden. There's no law that says you can't grow something productive in the front. Usually the back garden is where you and the family enjoy your leisure while the front is left as a decoration around the parking area. Amaze the neighbours when the lawn is replaced with cabbages.

Most modern gardens are surrounded with fences and a border, so rather than just decorative plants you can grow productive crops. When space is limited, it makes sense to grow crops that are expensive to buy and great to eat when fresh but also look attractive.

Think vertically!

One way to maximise production is to think vertically as well as horizontally. If you put tall plants on the outer edge by the fence, with ground-level plants in the border edging the lawn, you can get a surprising quantity from a very limited area.

Fruit trees can be trained up a fence. Apples, pears, apricots, peaches and especially cherries are easy and do well in this situation. Cherries are quite an expensive fruit to buy and Morello cooking cherries will grow well trained up a north-facing wall. Since most crops like plenty of sunshine, north-facing borders are least productive and cherries make good use of this resource.

Apricots and peaches should go on a sunny wall or fence to produce well. As they are very frost-sensitive you will need to cover them with fleece in spring, but otherwise they're not a lot of trouble.

If you've got a patio, a pergola over the top makes an ideal frame for supporting a grapevine. The large leaves provide shade in summer and the grapes hanging down look attractive as well.

It's not just fruits that can use vertical space: runner and climbing French beans produce a large crop for very little square footage. Don't forget that runner beans were originally used as a decorative plant. Amazingly people thought the beans were poisonous for many years, but eventually they learned differently. The variety Painted Lady has the most attractive flowers as well as producing a good crop.

Cordon tomatoes (those grown up a cane) are another productive plant that doesn't take a lot of room. While tomatoes are a bit of a hit-and-miss crop in the British climate, if you can provide shelter in spring and autumn you can get a crop, and those green tomatoes left at the end of the season make a fantastic chutney (see Chapter 7).

Going back to fruit, you may have seen those long bags that you hang up and produce a tower of flowers. Well, they can also grow quite a crop of strawberries. The great benefit to growing them like that is that the dreaded slugs and snails rarely find them.

And when it comes to hanging baskets, tumbler tomatoes do well in them. If you interplant with marigolds, the marigolds keep whitefly away (admittedly not too much of a problem), and make the basket look very decorative.

If you want a stunning architectural plant that would grace any TV gardening programme, plant a globe artichoke. They do take a lot of room, but they are an expensive delicacy and much more impressive than pampas grasses or bamboos.

Inter-planting the front of the border with mixed red and white cabbages can look impressive. Don't bother with those decorative cabbages though – they taste awful.

The real trick for getting a lot from a little space is never to have more empty space than absolutely necessary. If you can fit in a little cold frame somewhere – which can be knocked up easily from some scrap wood like old pallets and a couple of old window lights – then this will help no end in starting off crops early.

A greenhouse is useful, but if you haven't room for one don't worry. People grew crops before the invention of glass. If you can fit one in, do so. Keep an eye out in your local paper as they are available for peanuts second-hand. Often people just give them away.

Do try to take the old one down yourself if you can. This means you will know how it goes back together. Having built a lean-to greenhouse from wood and twin-wall polycarbonate myself from scratch, I saw a second-hand one free to take away the very next week. Patience is a virtue when keeping your costs down.

Don't buy new pots – reuse old containers

Sow successionally so that, as you harvest one crop, you have another plant growing on ready to take its place. Don't feel you need to spend money on pots and propagators, either. For pots there are all sorts of containers that we accumulate that will do the job perfectly well. Old margarine tubs, yogurt pots and even disposable cups can have a productive second life.

I noticed one of those awful automatic drink-vending machines at the car tyre centre with a bin full of used cups. They looked a little surprised when I asked if I could take them, but happily gave them to me. One hundred and fifty small pots for the price of asking. Even large pots can be picked up very cheaply. The supermarkets have their cut flowers delivered in small plastic buckets, which they then usually throw away. One charged 99p for eight of these 22cm (9in) plant pots; some give them away for the asking. You would be lucky to buy one pot that size for 99p, so either way it's a bargain.

For the large pot, just use an electric drill to pop some holes in the base. If you want holes in the small pots, which tend to be very flimsy, heat up a skewer or metal tent peg and burn them through. It's best done outside though as the smoke really stinks.

For propagators you can take a seed tray and make a framework from an old wire coat hanger to support a cover made from a clear plastic bag. Old 2-litre fizzy drink bottles can be made useful. Cut them across about a third of the way up. The bottom becomes a pot and the top is a little cloche which can be used on top of the soil or over a pot.

Even a paved courtyard can be made quite productive. Nearly anything you can grow in the ground can be grown in containers. In fact, some things like salad crops are better grown this way. It is easier to keep the slugs out of a container than off a plant in the border, for a start.

I deliberately say containers rather than pots as there are lots of things you can drum into service. That old galvanised bucket looks positively charming with plants growing from it. Even standard terracotta pots can be turned into something special by painting them. If you are, like me, artistically challenged, you can buy stencils quite cheaply and use those and a spot of paint to decorate your pots.

If you're trying to maximise production from a small space, or grow in containers, pay attention to the varieties you pick. Look at the seed merchants' catalogues or on their websites for descriptions that state 'suitable for close spacing' or 'close planting' or 'mini veg'. All of these mean the same thing: you can get more plants per square foot. Since a full-size cabbage will keep a family going for four meals or more, smaller crops can be a positive boon.

One expense you can really cut down on in the garden is the cost of seeds. Now I would always recommend buying good-quality seeds – although they do cost more than cheap seeds – but I think it's worth it because good crops come from good seeds and germination rates tend to be better in my experience. Having said that, with most seeds you get enough in the packet to last you for many seasons. Use what you want and store the rest in a dry, cool place – an airtight container in the fridge is the ideal – for the next year.

With many plants you can save your own seeds as well, so avoiding any cost at all. One gardener I know bought some shallots twenty years ago and hasn't bought any since. He keeps some back for the next season's crops.

I've covered the ins and outs of growing vegetables in my book *Vegetable Growing Month by Month* and more specifically allotment and larger plot growing in *The Essential Allotment*

Guide, both published in the Right Way series. There's also more information on my website: www.allotment-garden.org.

Making compost

Another way you can make your garden work for you is by recycling your kitchen and green waste. Most local councils offer subsidised compost bins – they look like tall dustbins – which make the job easy. It's surprising what can go into a compost bin: any green waste, of course, but also tea bags, crushed eggshells, coffee grounds, shredded paper, cardboard torn up small. You are converting your waste into a rich growing medium and helping the environment.

Although you needn't do more than add waste as it comes along, it's a good idea to alternately dust each 15cm (6in) deep layer with lime and nitrogen such as dried blood or sulphate of ammonia to speed up the process. Another way to add nitrogen is to water with urine diluted 10:1 (water to urine). It may not seem pleasant, but it is perfectly safe and human urine is sterile when supplied.

The bin is easily screened behind a few climbers, so don't worry about the appearance, but do allow room to get the contents out. There's usually a little door at the base to remove the compost, but that's useless. When it's full, lift the entire bin up vertically and put the uncomposted material at the top to one side.

Use the rest of the compost on your garden, replace the bin and put the unrotted material back in to restart the cycle.

As an alternative, many councils offer green waste bins where they will take your valuable raw materials away and convert them into compost, which they sell on. They even charge you for the privilege. Not my first option.

Wormeries

You can go a step further in converting waste for your benefit with a wormery. Basically the worms eat your food scraps and convert them into a high-quality soil nutrient. Now I know some people are quite revolted by worms, but honestly they won't hurt you – and without them our entire ecology would collapse.

You can buy worm-composting kits (and very sophisticated they are too) but they're easy to make yourself. All you need is a large plastic bin; an old-style dustbin is ideal. I've heard that the worms don't like the galvanised metal bins, so stick with plastic. Buy a water-butt tap and fit this as near to the base as possible, then fix a grill on the inside above the tap level. Weldmesh, available from hardware stores, is ideal. Cut to fit the inside at the right level and use two pieces run at right angles to keep the hole size small.

It should wedge into the slope of the bin, or support it on a couple of old bricks inside the bin. Now position your bin – somewhere warm is best, preferably frost-free – on some bricks so that you can get a can under the tap. In very cold weather, worms in the wild can burrow deep but they can't do that in your bin so insulate with bubble wrap or newspapers – anything to stop it freezing, which will certainly cramp your worms' style.

Then put about 7.5cm (3in) of gravel onto the mesh. This is going to allow the nutrient-rich liquids produced to collect under the mesh ready for you to drain off and use as a liquid plant food, while stopping the worms and compost from dropping down and blocking things up.

Next add a layer, about 7.5cm (3in) is fine, of compost or – better still – rotted farmyard manure. This is going to provide your worms with their food while they get established. Water this layer thoroughly with a can with a rose on the end.

Your next task is to add some worms. You need the fairly thin, red worms – they're called brandlings. You can find them in existing compost heaps or manure piles, but if you haven't a source then try a fishing tackle shop. There are specialist suppliers on the Internet, but a brandling worm is a brandling worm and the tackle shop should have live brandling worms. In fact, some people turn their wormeries into a part-time business, supplying fishing tackle shops.

Drop your worms into the bin and cover with a little more manure and a sheet of newspaper on the top, then lightly water. This stops things from drying out. Leave them alone for a week or two to get established.

All you have to do then is add your kitchen waste and the worms will convert it for you. Don't forget to drain off the liquid feed occasionally. When it fills to the top, dig out the contents down to the gravel layer and use that as a growing medium. Sort through and keep back a load of worms, then restart the cycle.

If you find your worms trying to climb out of the bin, the chances are it has become too acid. A little dusting of lime well watered in should cure it. Avoid putting in too much citrus peel, which is very acidic.

With both compost heaps and wormeries, avoid adding meat products, bones and foods like bread. These will attract vermin like rats and flies.

Biodigesters

In recent years we've seen biodigesters coming onto the market like Bokashi bins and the Green Cone food waste digester. The benefits of these are that they take up less room and can handle waste that you really shouldn't put onto the compost heap like dairy, meat products, cooking oils and cooked foods. They are not designed to cope with garden waste, so are not a replacement for the compost bin.

While I think they're a very green solution and worthwhile ecologically, there is the issue that you have to add activators to keep them working. It's really down to you to decide if you want to spend some money for the benefit of the ecology. You can be looking at £40 a year or more with a Bokashi system.

Don't forget to check for offers from your local authority. It helps them reduce their landfill so they often subsidise the cost of compost bins and digesters. I expect they'll be doing this more as the years go by.

The best compost bin I would recommend for a small garden is one called a Hotbin Composter. It's very well insulated and vermin proof so not only does it cope with garden waste but also food

CHAPTER 12 GROW YOUR OWN

waste, including small bones and meat. Even the contents of the cat litter tray can be safely added.

Used properly, it quickly heats up to 60°C (140°F) and makes great garden compost in a matter of a few weeks. They're quite expensive to buy but last for many years.

157

CHAPTER THIRTEEN

Keeping chickens

It is quite possible to keep some chickens properly in a small garden, and you'll save a little money by keeping your own hens for the eggs as well.

The poultry industry – a reality check

The poultry industry, like most of the food industry in the UK, is extremely efficient and produces both eggs and table birds at extremely low cost to the consumer. However, there is an awful welfare cost to this cheap food. If you've ever had the horrendous experience of visiting some intensive poultry farms, you will know that this is something we must stop. Although welfare standards have improved – with the introduction of larger cages for the birds, for example – just looking at the death rates for hens reared intensively for meat tells you there is something terribly wrong when around 1 in 20 die from injury and heart failure before being ready for the table.

Of course, the marketing men have come up with ways to disguise the treatment of the livestock, 'Fresh Farm Eggs' being a prime example. Fresh – well, yes, you don't want rotten eggs. Farm – when you read the word 'farm', do you think of a few hens scratching around in a yard or a whopping big industrial shed with tens of thousands of birds crammed into cages in a climate-controlled environment with conveyor belts taking out the eggs? Not quite the same, is it? A caged hen lives its entire short and wretched life on a wire-mesh floor in a rack, in a space little larger than a sheet of A4 paper.

Then we have 'Barn Eggs' – once again we're not talking about a few hens on a bale but another industrial building. But the hens do have the benefit of different levels, perching space and nesting boxes. One nest box per seven hens, crammed in at nine per square metre. Not far off two sheets of A4 per hen. Admittedly better than caged eggs, but not much – and certainly not luxury.

Due to public pressure most supermarkets now only sell free-range or organic-standard eggs, the caged eggs being sold to catering and food manufacturers. Free range and organic are by far the best systems, but even there not all is as good as we may hope for.

Free range, which is a legal definition, means the hens have 10 square metres per bird to roam in. This low density has the benefit of keeping the pasture in good condition with a low burden of worms and parasites. All well and good, but often the hens are in hangar-like sheds containing up to 16,000 birds.

In theory they have access to the pasture but many never actually get to push their way through the crush to the popholes and outside. In some ways the hens could be better off as colony caged birds without the stress.

Under UK organic standards, up to 2,000 laying hens or 1,000 table birds may be kept in a house, yet chickens naturally gather in small flocks. There is scientific research that shows they can recognise about fifty to sixty other birds and thereby maintain their pecking order.

No wonder that aggression becomes a problem when they are crammed in these huge numbers. The terrible practice of beak trimming is used to control this, but is not allowed under the Soil Association standards for organic husbandry. Beak trimming is banned in Sweden, Norway, Finland and Switzerland, but DEFRA almost promotes the practice to free-range producers. 'Free range' and 'organic' are clearly better than caged, but the reality is very different from what people believe it to be.

Incidentally, it's not just chickens. Ducks, turkeys and geese are all subject to similar conditions of dense stocking in large numbers.

This mistreatment of poultry is not the only reason to keep your own birds. There is scientific evidence that intensively reared chickens contain more fat and more of the harmful cholesterol-inducing fats than those allowed to range and develop more naturally.

The Soil Association has revealed that 12 per cent of non-organic eggs tested by the government in 2003 contained residues of lasalocid, a toxic antibiotic. Other residues, including chemicals not even approved for use on laying hens, have been found in eggs in the shops.

There is also scientific evidence that free-range eggs, where the birds actually get some of their nutrition from pasture, contain higher amounts of folic acid and vitamin B12 and vitamin A than caged eggs. Home-kept chickens, with a more varied diet than commercial free range, are most likely even better for us than that.

To be fair, when looking at the economics of keeping your own poultry you should compare the costs with those of organic eggs and meat, which are considerably higher than those produced under intensive systems. Or, to put it another way, you can enjoy the benefits of keeping your own hens and know that at worst it is not actually costing you anything to enjoy a superior product derived without cruelty – and you can even get a little profit.

Can you keep poultry?

Before deciding to keep poultry you need to consider a few points.

- Keeping poultry in the garden is rarely prohibited in the deeds of your house or by a local by-law. It would be unusual, but even if it is the case, if the birds are kept properly and cause no nuisance, you have to wonder who would report you or enforce that.
- Are you able to provide care every day? If you go away on holiday, then somebody must look after your birds. Unlike a dog, which can go to a boarding kennel, nobody runs holiday hotels for chickens!
- The family may all be in favour – and children will love the new pets – but your neighbours may not be so keen. Unless you have a cockerel (which isn't necessary) hens rarely crow

at dawn. It's worth explaining that before your hens arrive and the neighbours get out the protest placards.

- The other concern is that poultry attract rats and other vermin. The truth is that their food can do so, but proper management will prevent that. Food should be stored in rat-proof containers and you should avoid scattering too much food leaving excess for the vermin. That's inefficient anyway, and a lot of low-cost living is about being efficient.

- If you have a pet cat, chances are the cat will be somewhat scared of these giant sparrows stalking the garden. Usually a truce is declared after a week or two and the cat will studiously ignore these intruders. (If you have ever been ignored by a cat, you will know what I mean.) Do be aware, though, that what we see as cute fluffy chicks look like tasty snacks to a cat until they grow up into full-size hens. Cats only obey when you're looking, so don't rely on them remembering – because they won't.

- Dogs, unfortunately, can be a real problem and have the wherewithal to kill a hen easily. Even small dogs can show you they're not that far removed from a wolf at times. Luckily, dogs are more trainable and often you can bring out their shepherding side so that they'll protect your flock for you as if they were your children.

The economics of keeping laying hens at home

Back in 2006 I undertook a study of the costs involved and the returns for keeping hens at home based on half a dozen laying hens. This showed that I could realistically save around £200 a year on shop prices. Since then the price of feed has increased a little, but the price of free-range eggs in the shops has actually fallen – most likely due to the increased market size. Even organic eggs have hardly risen in price.

Despite that, you can still save between £100 and £150 a year on six birds producing eggs I would consider superior to anything you can buy in a shop, and kept at a higher welfare standard than organic.

If you're selling eggs at the gate (see page 172), it could be worth going for a lower-producing breed like the Araucana whose blue eggs attract a premium price, especially as they are said to be lower in cholesterol than other eggs.

What do you need to keep poultry?

Although it is possible to keep poultry indoors all the time, in a shed, say, they are happier when allowed access to the outside. Personally I think it is cruel to deprive any animal access to fresh air and at least some semblance of a natural environment.

Assuming they have access to the great outdoors, the accepted rule of thumb for housing is to allow just a square foot per bird. A small 120 × 90cm (4 × 3ft) house would be fine for twelve birds and a palace for six.

Larger breeds will need a little more space than smaller bantams, of course. The perching space is critical. If there is only room for five and you have six hens, this is a recipe for trouble.

If you just let your hens have the run of the garden they will love it. They'll scratch about eating slugs and other pests, dropping high-nitrogen fertiliser as they go and munching on the greenery. Unfortunately, 'the greenery' can include your prize flowers and vegetables.

Assuming your garden is securely fenced around the perimeter, the answer is temporary fencing to keep them from going where you don't want them, but they'll actually be happy with a run. Once again there is no set rule for this but a minimum run of around 20 square feet would be enough for four hens. That's just 150 × 120cm (5 × 4ft).

Although the free-range regulations demand stocking densities no higher than one bird per 10 square metres, in part this is required because it stops too much build-up of parasites and damage to grassland. However, the birds tend not to wander too far from the shed so the effective stocking density is much greater.

They will scratch up the soil and create dust baths for themselves, and in a short time the run will be devoid of vegetation. That's fine as long as you keep the run dry. Keeping the hens with wet feet all the time will cause you problems.

Another way to control them in the garden is to have, in addition to the permanent run, a movable run that you can put on the lawn and resite daily. Don't forget that chickens are jungle fowl and they don't like open skies too much. We know there aren't eagles here looking to swoop down on them, but they don't! They also don't like too much direct sunshine so shade is required. Some tarpaulin laid over one end of the run will provide enough cover, or place it under the shade of a tree.

You'll need a feeder and drinker but even brand new these will only cost a few pounds. If you pick up anything second-hand for your poultry, do ensure it is thoroughly cleaned and disinfected before use.

The biggest expense will be the housing, yet that need not cost much. You can go and buy a rather beautiful wooden ark painted in pastel colours or space-age plastic housing for many hundreds of pounds, but building your own is not that challenging to even the moderately handy. Technical plans are available to buy for just a few pounds, or you could go and look at a friend's coop and take notes.

For some reason you can often obtain rabbit hutches for less than equivalent-sized chicken coops. A bit of carpentry to add some perches and you have a chicken coop.

Another option is to use an existing shed. They don't require a lot of headroom or space so one side of the shed can be boxed in to just waist height and fitted out with perches, nestboxes, etc. With some thought, you can have a handy bench in your shed but don't forget that you'll need daily access to collect the eggs and weekly access to clean.

The important thing to note with a chicken house is that chickens need fresh air but loathe draughts. Provide ventilation, allowing air to flow above head height and they'll thrive, but allow draughts and you're in trouble.

Don't worry too much about keeping hens warm, within reason; they come with their own feather duvet. Hot weather is more debilitating than cold for them. As long as they are dry, protected from draughts and well fed, they will be fine.

Finally on housing: don't forget that foxes are more and more common in urban areas nowadays. Even in the middle of housing estates, you may well find an unwelcome visitor has been in the night so do ensure everything is secure.

So before running out with the chequebook, look at what resources you have to hand and what you can make for yourself. Thinking ahead and allowing time to find things second-hand is far more efficient and helpful for the frugal person.

If you want, there's no reason to stop at a few hens. You can keep ducks quite easily in a normal back garden. They need access to water for preening but a small pond or even a half barrel sunk into the ground will be enough for them.

What stock to get and where to find it

Your first job is to decide what type of hen to get. There's a bewildering number of breeds, some best for eggs, some for meat, some make good mothers and some more for show. Some are hardier than others and some make good all-rounders. Some are better for beginners and others more demanding. All this choice is a bit confusing but, to simplify, the traditional pure breeds have their qualities but for quantity of eggs you really need to go for a hybrid.

Silkies are popular for their amazing looks with their almost fur-like feathers, but lay only around a hundred smallish eggs a year if you are lucky. These are really pets with the bonus of some eggs.

The traditional Welsummer is a friendly hen – good if you have children – but we're only looking at around 140 eggs a year, so not terribly profitable, whereas the Wyandotte is more likely to donate 200 eggs a year and still has a good nature. The Rhode Island Red is both calm and hardy, producing around 200 eggs a year, so again it's good for the beginner. The Araucana can be worth keeping as they lay greenish-blue eggs, which can command a premium price.

It's interesting to note how at one time white-shelled eggs were considered pure, but then became associated with battery rearing and the battery producers switched to brown-egg-laying breeds which were associated in the public mind with free-range hens. The truth is that the eggshell colour depends on the breed, not how they are kept.

The Black Rock is quite a productive hybrid that copes well with free ranging, often producing 250 eggs a year, but for sheer production, whether of eggs or for table, you need a modern hybrid breed like the Amber Link. Egg production is near double that of many of the pure, traditional breeds, often exceeding 300 a year.

You can buy your hens at different ages from day old or even as fertile eggs to incubate yourself. As a rule, the younger the bird the cheaper it is. For the beginner after laying hens, the best stage to buy is a point-of-lay pullet. A pullet is a hen in the first year of life when it is most productive.

After the first season egg production drops by about 20 per cent, in the second and third years dropping away more gradually. Point of lay is about 16–18 weeks old when the hen is ready to start laying.

Hens do not require a cockerel (male bird) to start laying or produce eggs thereafter (unless you want the eggs to be fertile for breeding). Make sure you're only buying hens or you'll be treating the neighbourhood to a dawn chorus at cockcrow.

Having decided what you want, you need to find a fairly local, reputable breeder. Local papers, poultry magazines and my website, www.lowcostliving.co.uk, carry lists of breeders. Prices can vary and, as with everything, there are rogues out there, but the vast majority of small poultry breeders are in it for the hobby, not the money.

Another option well worth considering is to contact one of the rescue charities and obtain some ex-battery hens. These will cost very little (£1 is common, but some are cashing in with higher prices) and obviously these birds are from productive hybrid stock. The producers find it more economical to change their stock after a year as production falls and sell the birds on for pet food, despite them having productive years of life left.

When you get them, they will look awful. Feathers will be missing, almost bald in places. They will be bewildered and hardly know how to walk. It's heartbreaking. Yet it's a testament to their strength and spirit how quickly most take to a new life and the freedom to move about. Their natural instincts reassert themselves and after a few months you would hardly know they've spent a year in a concentration camp.

Sadly you do need to be prepared for a fairly high mortality rate initially. Some just can't cope with the change and seem to die of shock. If you have children, you may want to keep this in mind and prepare them.

Feeding your hens

The wild jungle fowl from which our hens are descended literally scratched a living from the forest floor. They lived on insects, seeds and shoots, and that was sufficient for a bird laying perhaps a dozen eggs a year.

Our modern hens are a triumph of the breeder's art. They efficiently convert food into meat and eggs for us, but a scratched living is no longer enough to sustain their rate of egg production. To lay a 50g (2oz) egg nearly every day, the hen needs 100g (4oz) of food, which is about the capacity of her crop. This has to provide the required amount of protein, carbohydrate and oils or egg production and the health of the hen will suffer. Just like a sports car with a highly tuned engine, a high-producing breed of hen needs high-octane fuel to perform.

If you have a modern hybrid hen producing 250 eggs plus a year then you'll be best to just feed on quality layers pellets. With pure breed hens who produce fewer eggs, and so have lower nutritional needs, you can replace some of the pellets with free food like home-grown greens.

Bored hens have a tendency to start pecking at each other and you'll be surprised at the damage their beaks can inflict. I've seen hens make short work of a mouse in a run and they devoured it in minutes.

Hanging some greens in the run, perhaps a cabbage past its best or a bolted lettuce, will not only provide them some fresh green food but also something more interesting to peck than each other. If you find slugs and snails in the garden, dump them into the run as well; it's all good protein.

In years gone by, vegetable peelings, stale bread, plate leavings and green waste like the outer leaves and stalk of brassicas all went into a stockpot to be boiled and shredded into a mash to provide a supplement to bought-in feed. Under British legislation this is now illegal. Basically any food that has gone through the kitchen should not be fed to your poultry. If you cut off the excess leaves from your cabbage outside, before taking it into the kitchen, that's legal. Cut them off in the kitchen and you can get two years in clink, in theory. It's a mad old world.

Don't buy from pet stores. You want a supplier geared more for the smallholder. Internet suppliers can be worth checking too, despite carriage costs. It's important to store your food carefully to keep it dry and in good condition. If you store it in a shed, then invest in an old-fashioned metal dustbin with a lid. The plastic ones are fine but if you get a rat about, he'll chew through the plastic in short order. We use an old broken small chest freezer to store our chicken feed.

Table (meat) birds

If you raise your own birds for the table you will have the pleasure of knowing that they've been treated humanely and had a decent life up until the evil day, unlike those birds from the broiler house system. But this raises two major questions: can you bring yourself to kill your own birds and, having killed them, can you eat them?

It's one thing to say you can kill your bird when the time comes, but the kids named her Perky and she's looking at you trustingly. Only you can answer that question. Even if you can kill her, what will the family say? It's no use sitting down to a meal of roast chicken with the children crying their eyes out because you murdered Perky. (Actually children seem, in my experience, to be remarkably easy about the whole thing, but they all differ.)

I don't believe a book can really teach you how to kill a bird humanely, but it is something you should know if only to handle culling an injured bird to prevent suffering. If you find a local poultry keeper who is rearing for the table, he or she is the best person to ask to teach you.

If you are faced with an emergency situation like a badly injured bird after an encounter with a fox, then I would suggest decapitation with a sharp axe or cleaver. Be calm, firm and above all decisive. Don't hesitate or half do it.

The immediate severing of the spinal column and massive pressure loss to the brain means death is effectively instantaneous. Nobody can say painless with certainty, but having once collapsed from low blood pressure, I think it is.

The wings will flap and headless birds have been known to run around – that's where the phrase 'run around like a headless chicken' comes from. This is all down to the autonomic nervous system, and not a sign of actual life.

What to do with all those eggs!

If, as a family, you get through a dozen eggs a week, then you might well assume that's about 600 a year and so three hens will suffice. Nature, however, is not quite so regimented.

The hen's laying pattern is defined by the day length, and while she may give you an egg a day in the summer, come the dark days of winter you may only get one or two each week. You can extend the laying by providing artificial light to the house, but do you really want to push your hens so hard?

The net result is that you will have gluts and shortages. Your eggs will keep well in a fridge at around 5°C (41°F) for a couple of months. Keeping them on the side in a warm kitchen will reduce that time considerably, in a hot summer perhaps to as little as a week. Just take the eggs out of the fridge an hour or two before you need to use them.

For longer-term storage you can freeze eggs, but not in their shells which would crack as the contents expanded. You can use the trays for making ice cubes. You'll find that the yolk fills one cube and the white two, which is useful for judging how many eggs you are using when the time comes.

The traditional methods of storing eggs – painting, waterglass and salting – are all a lot more fuss and difficult than simply freezing.

Another good way to store them is to make pickled eggs, a swappable or saleable product. You might sell your eggs at 20p each but pickled eggs have added value so you might get 50p an egg if they're in a nice jar with an attractive label.

Pickled eggs

- Place your eggs in a saucepan with cold water and bring to the boil. Don't put them into boiling water as it can cause blue rings in the eggs. If you stir the eggs gently during the first few minutes of boiling, it helps to centralise the yolks in the white.
- Once hard-boiled, cool them slightly in cold water, then remove the shell and pack into clean, sterilised jars while still hot.
- Pour over hot spiced vinegar, cover and label and store when cold. You can buy pickling vinegar or make your own by putting a bag of pickling spice into vinegar and bringing it to the boil. Switch off the heat, remove the bag and pour over the eggs.

If you make your own spiced vinegar you can use cider vinegar if you prefer, which is milder, or you can add a chilli pepper to add a little zing. Experiment and who knows what you will come up with!

Selling your eggs

To be clear, we're talking about selling surplus eggs here, not commercial production. As your production goes up to business levels the regulatory burden grows, but for a few home-produced eggs you rely on an exception technically known as 'Farm Gate Sales'.

Even with farm gate sales of eggs (for the sake of argument, your house is the farm here) there are still some rules that you need to follow.

- **Ungraded (not sized) eggs** The eggs cannot be split into sizes or quality grades, although you might choose to keep the largest and smallest for yourself and just offer the rest. Do remember that people buying eggs from the farm gate may well like different sizes in one box. It can be very useful when cooking to be able to use a small egg or a large one, depending on the recipe.

- **Quality** The eggs you offer should be clean, but not washed. Most buyers of farm eggs will not be too bothered by a spot of poo on the eggshell, but technically you should reserve those for your own use.

- The eggshells should not be damaged or cracked. A cracked egg has its protection against microbes damaged and should be reserved for your own use and used as quickly as possible, preferably within a day or two of laying.

- **Freshness and best before dates** You need to display a 'best before' date to comply with the law. Usually eggs are expected to last up to four weeks from the date of laying and you should (hopefully) be selling them within a day or two of lay. If you keep your excess eggs in boxes, use some system to date order them so you never accidentally sell old eggs.

- A sign saying 'Best Before Three Weeks from Date of Purchase' will keep you legal.

Marketing your eggs

Don't worry – I'm not suggesting you hire an advertising agency and survey focus groups, but you do need to tell people what you're selling.

- **First you need to put up a sign**, large enough to be easily read from the road and positioned so it can be easily seen. Remember a car may be doing 30mph so it needs to be large enough to be read in the time that whizzes by. Not a billboard though!

- If you find sign painting daunting, print your sign on paper using your computer, then cover with cling film or laminate to stop it washing away in a shower. Keep it simple – '**Eggs For Sale**' says it all. In smaller letters add a message like '**Just Knock on the Door**' or '**House up the Path, Just Knock on the Door**'. Many people are reticent to walk up a private drive and knock. I know it seems a bit unnecessary but, trust me, it tells people they are welcome.

- Another good tip is to have a second sign under the top one which is on hooks and can be changed saying '**Eggs in Stock**' or '**Sorry Sold Out Today**'. This does two things: it tells customers they are not wasting their time coming up your drive; also if they see 'sold out' it tells them your eggs are really fresh, encouraging them to come back.

- **Be careful about claims** Avoid using descriptive terms like 'organic' or 'free range'. These are legal terms and you may need to prove your status legally. If someone asks, offer to show them your hens. Once they see your hens and you explain why you hate battery keeping, you will have a customer for life.

- **Generating customers for your eggs** If the sign doesn't raise enough interest to move your surplus eggs, perhaps you're too far off the beaten track. You'll need to build up a customer base. The best method is word of mouth. If you have a load of excess eggs and you're not going to be able to sell them – give some away. If someone buys a dozen eggs, give them an extra half-dozen and tell them to tell their friends.

- **Advertising is pretty pointless** and certainly not cost-effective but a few leaflets in the locality will help. If you're hard to find, then a little map can work wonders, along with a phone number if customers get lost.

Further information

There's no substitute for meeting up with others who keep poultry and learning from them. Our book *Backgarden Chickens and Other Poultry* goes into the subject in depth, and there's a wealth of information on the Internet, of course.

My www.chickens.allotment-garden.org website has a large and popular section on keeping poultry, as well as a busy chat area where people ask for and give advice.

CHAPTER FOURTEEN

Bees in the back garden

Keeping bees has always been considered a country pursuit – the country cottage garden with a beehive at the bottom and the bees harvesting pollen from the flowers. In fact, they're very suitable for keeping in a town garden. The basic food for bees is pollen from the flowers and town gardens are full of those.

Sadly, the countryside is not as good for keeping bees as the town nowadays. Look around and you'll see endless acres of flowerless fields growing crops. Worse than that, the regular use of pesticides and herbicides has contributed to the decimation of our bee population. This general reduction in the number of bees is a terrifying prospect as they are vital to our ecology and food production.

Although bees are incredibly productive creatures for the beekeeper, they also serve a vital role in our ecology. As they fly around collecting pollen they fertilise the flowers. This is necessary for crop production. Without bees to pollinate, our agriculture would be in a sorry state.

All the legumes (that's peas and beans) depend on bees for a start. And if you kept the bees out of your greenhouse, then you'd find you wouldn't get a crop of tomatoes; it's the bees that pollinate the plants.

In the USA there is a large industry of beekeepers taking their hives up and down the country just to fertilise orchards and crops. Many self-sufficiency enthusiasts who have taken to keeping bees have noted improved crops just due to improved pollination rates. Busy bees, indeed!

Where to site the hive

You don't need much room to keep bees – a hive only takes up a few square feet – but you do need enough room or the right place to keep them safely. You can't just plonk a hive on the lawn where the children play football; if the ball hits the hive you'll have a few thousand very agitated bees looking for trouble.

So the first rule must be to site the hive somewhere that can be secured to prevent curious young children from gaining unsupervised access. Your bees will be flying back and forth so you need to consider their flight path. If the flight path is across the lawn-cum-football pitch, someone is bound to get stung eventually. Unlike wasps, bees die when they sting, so they're not naturally aggressive – but waving your arms around to drive them off tends to provoke them.

There is a relatively easy answer to the flight-path problem: surround the area of the hive with a fence or hedge about 2m (6ft) high. The bees will leave the hive and fly up to get over the barrier, above the heads of your football team.

Because they fly, you can think three-dimensionally about where the hive is sited. Perhaps you have a flat roof on an extension or garage. The bees will then happily go back and forth way above everyone's head.

Costs and benefits

Unlike hens, where you can reasonably predict the number of eggs each year, bees are more dependent on the weather. They hibernate in the winter so a long winter or a slow start to the spring means fewer flowers to feed them and less time to produce honey.

Since towns and cities tend to be a few degrees warmer than the open countryside, the effect is to moderate winter temperatures and bring spring forward. Another advantage for the urban beekeeper.

The yield of honey per hive will on average be around 13.5kg (30lb), but you could see double that in a good year. On the other hand, you could see nothing in a terrible year, but thankfully that is fairly rare.

The economics of beekeeping will obviously depend on the year and your yield. As with many things, economies of scale play a part. You need as much equipment to tend one hive as half a dozen. Buying new equipment from a budget supplier for three hives will set you back upwards of £450 (and that can be well upwards). You'll also need to get your bees and they can cost near £200. If you can find equipment second-hand you can bring the investment down, of course. Like all livestock, once you have your first stock you can breed your own as well.

The actual running costs are fairly low, but this is not a hobby which will provide a fast return.

What price you can sell your honey for will affect your profit, of course. Don't forget that an attractive label can be worth a pound a jar in the buyer's mind. With desktop publishing programs even the graphically challenged can produce very professional labels.

You're not limited to simply selling honey in jars. There's a market for cosmetic products incorporating honey: shampoos, face cream, hand cream and soap. Because you're adding value to your product, the returns are far greater.

Your product range is wider than just the honey as well. Beeswax is a saleable product but home-made beeswax candles and furniture polish are more profitable.

Beeswax polish is simple to make.

- Start with equal amounts of turpentine and beeswax. You need real turpentine (not turpentine substitute), so you may have to look around a bit to find it.

- Grate the beeswax and put it into a jar, and add your turpentine. A Kilner jar is ideal, having a wide neck and lid.
- Eventually (usually after a week or so) the wax will have dissolved into the turpentine.
- You can speed things up by putting the jar into a pan of hot water. Be very careful with heating turpentine: it's highly flammable, especially when warm. No smoking rules apply. Keep the lid on the jar as well when heating or the turpentine vapours escape. If the mix ends up too hard, add a little more turpentine; if too sloppy, leave the lid off and it will harden.
- Adding a few drops of lemon oil or other aromatic oil like orange or lavender will add a pleasant smell to the product. You can buy 100ml tins, like shoe-polish tins, to pack your polish in.

Keeping bees is a fascinating hobby and can really make a contribution to your budget eventually, but you need to do your homework. Spend some time with a local beekeeper and decide if it is for you before rushing out with your chequebook.

Further information

Keeping bees is something to consider carefully before jumping in, and it's obviously beyond the scope of this book to go into all the ins and outs if it. A visit to your local bookshop or library is called for, and you should also contact a local beekeeper for some hands-on experience and guidance.

The British Beekeepers' Association will be able to help and put you in touch with local beekeepers and associations.

British Beekeepers' Association

The National Beekeeping Centre

National Agricultural Centre

Stoneleigh Park

Warwickshire

CV8 2LG

www.britishbee.org.uk

CHAPTER FIFTEEN

Pets

By 'pets' I'm really talking about dogs and cats since they're what we know best, and what are most commonly kept. You can save money by doing some good and taking on a rescued animal. Pedigree dogs and cats not only cost a lot of money to buy, but they often cost a fortune to keep. Sadly such animals have been designed for their looks and in the process genetic defects have also been bred in. The moggy or the mutt tends to be healthier and they often have a better personality as well.

Kittens and puppies are great fun for a few months until they grow up, but what a lot of trouble. Stepping into an 'accident' is no joke when you get up, and watching the kittens race up the curtains, shredding them in the process, soon loses its charm. Slightly older animals need homes too and you get the years of companionship without the initial pain. Contact an animal rescue charity like the Cats Protection League or RSPCA.

I'd recommend pet insurance for young animals. In the first years they're most likely to have an accident or develop an illness. Vet's fees can be horrendous, and although the PDSA will provide help for those receiving financial help through either Housing Benefit or Council Tax Benefit and who live in a practice's catchment area, if you are not eligible you may be faced with a choice between debt or putting your pet to sleep.

If you find yourself paying for long-term treatments (as we did with an elderly cat), then you can save a lot of money by buying the pills online. The vet will provide a prescription for which he will charge, and which the online pharmacy accepts before dispatching the drugs. Be straight with your vet. He'd rather keep a customer and your pet alive than lose both of you as clients.

Incidentally, the online suppliers in the UK are strictly regulated by the Veterinary Medicines Directorate who ensure the quality of their premises, procedures, drug quality and the content of their site. If in doubt about a website you should find their physical address on the site and a telephone contact, usually on an 'About us' or 'Contact us' page. If they are based in the UK you are safe.

Make your own pet food

We've got five cats, so feeding them costs more than feeding us, and we wanted to bring the costs down. Amazingly, it pays us to buy their biscuits online in bulk. Always try a small quantity first before buying a large bag, as cats are notoriously fussy creatures.

You've probably noticed that the pet food manufacturers are producing more and more sachets. Compare the cost of four sachets with one can and you'll find canned food is a lot cheaper, but you can do better than that. We've actually found tinned pink salmon cheaper than tinned cat food, so there's room for some savings. Incidentally, the tinned salmon wouldn't be a good everyday food as cats and dogs need vitamins that pure meat doesn't contain.

It is possible to make your own pet food at a fraction of the cost of tinned pet foods, and these are also of benefit to pets with a sensitive digestive tract. Just like us, dogs and cats need vitamins. In the wild they don't just eat meat; they also eat the contents of their prey's stomachs, which provides some vegetable matter in the diet.

The pet food manufacturers cover this need by adding vitamins, and we need to do the same to keep our pets healthy. You can buy powdered multi-vitamins (SF50 being the one we use) easily and cheaply online.

Cats require more natural protein sources from meat or fish than dogs, with a balance of 60 per cent meat, 20 per cent vegetables, 20 per cent starch. Dogs require a different balance of 40 per cent meat, 30 per cent vegetables, 30 per cent starch. The starch should be from sources such as brown rice and not from wheat sources. A selection of vegetables helps the dog's 'five a day' nutritional balance.

If you change your pet's diet, do so gradually to avoid gastrointestinal upsets and your pet rejecting the new diet – although our cats much prefer home-made to shop food.

The recipes below have been a success with our cats and could be easily adapted for dogs by changing the proportions, reducing the meat to vegetables and starch ratio. They can be made in bulk and frozen in portion sizes, or made fresh and kept in the fridge for up to three days. Don't be afraid to experiment a bit, especially if you find some meat or poultry reduced to clear in the shop. Just stick to the proportions covered above. Don't add any salt or seasonings.

Liver and kidney cobbler

For cats that prefer stronger flavours or are elderly and need a stronger smell from their food to get them to eat, this is a good mixture.

- Cook 600g (1lb 3oz) liver and kidney 50/50 mix (ideally pig's kidney and liver as this is stronger smelling) with 200g (7oz) brown rice and 200g (7oz) vegetables (root vegetables, leafy greens or Sunday night's leftover veggies can be used as long as they are varied). Place all ingredients into a large cooking pot and just cover with water.
- Bring to the boil and then simmer for 20 minutes before draining off any excess water.
- Add 15g (1tbsp) of a good-quality multivitamin (such as SF50 for cats) after cooking, then blend the mixture in a processor until smooth.

This creates a mix very similar to expensive cat pâtés and a portion should be about 3tbsp per cat per meal, split between three meals a day. This should be reduced if adding dry food, with 20g ($^3/_4$ oz) dry food such as biscuits accounting for a 3tbsp serving. Having said that, I feed a poorly cat as much as I can.

Fishy surprise

Again a strong-smelling food that can be used to encourage sick cats to eat and that is gentle on sensitive stomachs. Most major supermarkets do a value or budget frozen pack of mixed fish that is economical and excellent for home-made cat food. We had a friend who ran a chip shop and asked him if he would sell us some uncooked fish, explaining why. He told us he had loads of misshapen fillets and cuts that we could have for free. Always worth asking in your chip shop.

- Cook 500g (1lb) white fish with 100g (4oz) brown rice, 225g (8oz) potatoes with skins and 200g (7oz) vegetables. Place all ingredients into a large cooking pot and cover with water.
- Boil and then simmer for 20 minutes before draining any excess water.
- Add 15g (1tbsp) of SF50 (for cats) after cooking, then blend the mixture until smooth.
- Add to this mixture a small tin of boneless sardines in olive oil, cut into small pieces, and a small tin of drained tuna in brine.

Cats love this just as much as premium fish cat foods.

CHAPTER SIXTEEN
Cleaning

If you watch the TV adverts you could be forgiven for believing we are a nation obsessed with cleanliness living in a world of filth. The range of different products in the supermarket would have filled the corner shop of yesteryear.

You're told that your kitchen worktops and chopping board have more germs than a toilet seat (and I sincerely hope that isn't the toilet in the bathroom cleaning adverts!). The implication usually is that if you don't buy this product or that, then not only will your friends shun you but your children will die and it's all your fault.

The truth is obvious: you don't need fifty different cleaning products, and it's perfectly possible to maintain a high standard of cleanliness without them. There are a lot of ecologically better and financially cheaper alternatives you can use.

We've become paranoid about germs and happily buy anti-bacterial cleansers, yet we seem to forget we already have a powerful and cheap bactericide in the cupboard: ordinary bleach.

The active ingredient in bleach is sodium hypochlorite, and there's very little difference between the amount in different bleaches. As well as splashing around the toilet, adding an eggcupful to a bucket of water with a squirt of washing-up liquid makes an effective bactericidal floor cleanser when mopping.

On the subject of bacteria, one of the worst offenders in the kitchen is the dishcloth. Being damp, and with bits of food in the fibres, it is an almost perfect culture dish for germs. Rinse and hang it up at night. We drape it over the tap and it dries out, which reduces the bacteria count tremendously. Every few days, soak it overnight in the bowl with just a squirt of bleach and it will be sterile and clean.

Mixing bicarbonate of soda with white vinegar makes a fantastic cleaner. We put 2tbsp bicarb with 2tbsp vinegar into a pint of water along with a splash of lemon juice and $1/2$ tbsp salt. Pour it into a spray bottle that once held a commercial product and we have our own spray cleaner that cuts through grease in a flash.

Both bicarbonate of soda and vinegar are excellent cheap natural cleaners. A little bicarb sprinkled on a cloth will clean as well as most cream cleaners, and a tablespoon of vinegar in a pint of water makes a great window cleaner. Dry off with crumpled newspaper for a perfect shine.

Don't buy your bicarb in those fiddly little jars in the baking section of the shop; you can get 500g (1lb) packs for under £2 on eBay. You need distilled white vinegar (often used for pickling) for cleaning, not malt vinegar which smells like chips. You can buy it cheaply in the supermarket.

Cleaning the oven used to be the worst job in the house. Whether we used sprays or those pads you prick with the pin, the fumes were awful. Now we mix about 170g (6oz) of washing soda with 1tbsp salt and mix with a little water to turn it into a paste.

Spread this over the inside of the oven and just leave until the next day when it washes off along with all the burnt grease. Washing soda is chemically similar to baking soda (bicarbonate of soda) but much stronger. Don't confuse the two.

If you go into most professional kitchens you'll find steel wool by the washing up sink. It's cheap to buy, lasts for years and is great for cleaning things like burnt-on deposits on pans. Add a little bicarb and the toughest grill pan can be tackled in minutes.

Both bicarb and washing soda are well-known chemicals that have been in use for a few hundred years. Far less expensive to buy, no side effects (unless you eat the washing soda!) and you're not adding cocktails of chemicals to your house. They make real sense.

Washing clothes

We're probably wearing cleaner clothes now than our ancestors would have ever imagined. Shirts worn but once go into the wash, despite being perfectly clean to the naked eye. In fact, most of the average washing basket looks fine, but we want to freshen them up more than scrub grime out of them.

Back before the Clean Air Acts when everyone had coal fires, the air (and the inside of the house) was full of soot and smuts. Now we've cleaned up our environment, our clothes just don't get as dirty as they did.

For these relatively clean clothes, just put them on the shortest wash at the lowest temperature without any powder. I promise nobody will ever know. We're seeing adverts for detergents all the time promising brilliant results at lower temperatures, but strangely they never suggest you might not even need the washing powder!

A friend of ours has a child who suffers from eczema. She stopped using powders altogether and not only did the eczema clear up, nobody noticed any difference in the cleanliness of the washing either.

EcoBalls®

We spend a fortune on detergents – basically washing soda with a few extra chemicals – to wash our clothes, but there are alternatives. Even your dirtier clothes need not use any powder. Consider buying some EcoBalls®. You just put the balls into the washing machine instead of soap powder. They contain pellets made of mineral salts that produce ionised oxygen which acts like a powder. They cost about £30 but will do a thousand washes before you need a refill kit that costs about £20. They also work well on short, cool wash cycles.

Soap nuts

There's one more cleaning product I really would recommend. It's completely natural, ecologically sound, helps impoverished Third World farmers and it's cheap. That has to be as good as it gets.

Soap nuts/pods are in fact a berry found in India and Nepal. They are harvested sustainably from the soap berry tree and the shells are then dried for use as they are a natural source of saponins, a soap-like chemical.

The pods can be purchased from a variety of online retailers and on average cost £12 including delivery for 1kg (2.2lb), which equates to approx. 750 pods. They usually come in a large drawstring cotton bag with a smaller cotton bag for use in the washing machine.

The pods don't release harmful chemicals into your home or the environment. Soap pods are very good for people with dry skin or eczema and due to the lack of chemicals reduce inflammation and itchiness, which is often associated with using conventional detergents.

To wash clothes you use four to six pods in the small wash bag and these can be used for three to five washes, working out at a cost in the region of 3p per wash (compared to the equivalent estimated 25p per wash with a standard non-bio powder).

They can be used at any temperature and for any wash type, including delicates and wool. Although the soap nuts have a natural vinegar smell before use, once placed in the wash with your clothes they are odourless. There is no need to add fabric softener, but if you like scented clothing add a couple of drops of your favourite essential oil to either the wash bag or into your washer draw.

Once the pods have been used and have turned brown/soggy do not throw them away. Store them in an airtight container until you have collected sixty pods and they can then be used for other purposes (see below).

Household cleaner

Once you have collected around sixty pods, put them in a pan and add 1 litre (2 pints) water. Bring to the boil and then simmer for 10 minutes and then just leave to cool. Once cool, strain the liquid and add 10 drops of tea tree oil (a natural disinfectant which can be purchased online for circa £3.50 for 10ml [1^{1}/$_{2}$ tsp] and which will last for up to six months of use) and then decant into old spray bottles saved from household chemical sprays and detergents.

This will last for up to one month and can be used for the kitchen, bathroom and as a floor wash. Add 1tsp white vinegar and use it to clean glass and metal surfaces to a shine, or add a little vinegar and baking soda and use to clean your toilet bowl. This mixture, with no additives, can also be used to soak clothes with stubborn stains before adding them to the normal clothes wash as described above.

Personal care

Make up your liquid as above, but add 10ml (1^{1}/$_{2}$ tsp) of your favourite essential oil for scent. Tea tree oil works well for skin prone to spots and blemishes; orange oil for sensitive skin; bergamot for dry skin; or maybe camomile for aches and pains and to relax.

This can be added to your bathwater, used as a body wash and hand wash or as shampoo for up to a month after making.

Although it will not lather in the same way as conventional products it cleans just as well and for a fraction of the cost, and at no cost to you or the environment as it does not add further excess chemicals to waste water or to your body.

For a natural conditioner try adding 1tsp of olive oil to the mixture and rub through your hair, paying particular attention to the ends, and then rinse out as normal.

CHAPTER SEVENTEEN

Energy

We're exhorted to save energy and reduce our carbon emissions – which is good advice – but some of the methods I've seen suggested make no economic sense or even any sense in terms of actually doing the job. If more carbon is created in producing an energy-saving gadget than it saves over its lifetime, then this is not green in any way.

Cutting the cost

Before we look at energy saving, though, are you paying too much for it anyway? It is worth spending half an hour checking that you are getting the best deal for gas and electricity prices. There are a number of websites where you can punch in your information and they will tell you what deals are on offer.

For some reason the energy companies like to make things really complicated. Their rates vary according to your usage and where you live, and they have a bewildering array of plans. One has to wonder if they hope you'll just give up in confusion and do nothing.

Some offer fixed-rate deals. These are good if you expect rates to go up, but not so good if rates fall. Although the long-term (ten years) outlook is only upwards, in the short term who knows? We've seen oil double in price then fall back to less than half in a matter of months – and oil is the driver of the energy market and the price we pay for gas and electricity.

Before you go online, get out last year's bills. The website questionnaires will ask how much energy you use to select the best deal for you. If you're intending to make some efficiency improvements, pump in last year's figures and then the same again less 20 per cent in case the recommendation changes.

It's worth checking on a couple of websites, just in case one gives a better option than another. Take a look at these:

- www.energyhelpline.com
- www.theenergyshop.com
- www.uswitch.com

Don't forget to check your bills against your meter as well. The estimated bills they send out can mean you're overpaying – not good – or underpaying. Then one day a huge bill arrives and you could have problems settling it. Check you're on the most appropriate tariff for your type of usage as well, as that can make a significant difference.

While on the subject of meters, be aware that with gas there are two types: older ones measure in cubic feet and modern ones in cubic metres. If your supply is charging you for cubic feet and your meter is in cubic metres, you can be paying far too much. To quickly check, divide the number of kWhs by the number of gas units. It should come to about 11; if it's about 33 then you are being charged for an imperial meter instead of a metric one and should contact your supplier for a large rebate.

Insulation

Heating is the largest use of energy in the home, so this obviously gives us the best opportunity to save money and reduce those carbon emissions. The television programmes show all sorts of wonderful green energy-saving ideas, ventilation systems that transfer heat from stale to fresh air being just one. Now this is an effective technology for a large office building but it makes no sense at all for the man in the street, unless he lives in a twenty-bedroom mansion!

The most cost-effective and easy ways to stop heat escaping are not particularly exciting but they will save you money in a reasonable time – and reduce that carbon footprint.

It's also possible to get government grants for improving the energy efficiency of your home. Check out what's available before you start. The website www.energysavingtrust.org.uk has a wealth of useful information.

Draughtstripping

Wooden exterior doors and windows tend to warp a little and the wind whips through, but you can buy rolls of sticky-backed foam strips for a couple of pounds and apply it in just a few minutes. It will only take an afternoon to sort out all your windows and doors (and that's with a long tea break). For the bottom of the doors you can fix a flexible brush strip so it will still ride over the floor.

Don't forget the letterbox; you can get a draught-proof cover for that. Check the cat flap as well; it can pay to replace a poorly fitted flap.

Check if you can draught-proof the loft hatch. You might not notice the draught up at ceiling level but your expensively heated air can be warming your loft space, and from there the world.

One area where you may be surprised to find a draught is around the windows. There's little point in having energy-efficient, double-glazed windows and let the heat leak out around the sides. If you have draught-proofed and can still feel a draught, check again. Luckily it is easily and cheaply fixed by using a flexible silicone sealant, applied with a gun around the exterior edges. To avoid it sticking to your finger when you smooth it, put a drop of washing-up liquid on your finger first. If there are cracks on the inside, decorator's filler applied the same way and then painted over will fix them.

When you're sitting in the nice warm living room and a draught is coming under the door from the cold hallway, why not use an old-fashioned 'sausage' to block it? They're easily made by stuffing a fabric tube. Sew on some feet, eyes and a nose and you've got a sausage dog soft toy that's useful as well as amusing.

Loft insulation

Back in the days before anyone really thought about climate change and fuel was cheap, the recommendation was 100mm

(4in) of loft insulation. So we take a look up in the loft, see some squashed-down fibreglass under the cobwebs and dust and think we're fine. A quarter of your heating bill escapes through the loft and really you want about 300mm (12in) depth, so it's well worth topping up that old insulation.

There are different types of insulation available: fibre fills that are blown between the joists and foam sprays that go under the tiles (and can help fix a leaking roof at the same time). For a DIY job, fibreglass rolls are the easiest route but do wear a mask, gloves and goggles. It's horrible prickly stuff and can really irritate for days after.

Don't insulate under any water tanks, or they might freeze. If you're left with any exposed water pipes above the insulation, lag them as well.

Your payback on loft insulation will usually be a year or less, with a tonne of carbon emissions saved each year as well.

Cavity-wall insulation

Next on the list of cost-effective energy savers is to have the cavity walls filled. It's not really a DIY job so shop around and check out a company who will undertake the work. You should get an insurance-backed guarantee as well from reputable companies.

The work usually only takes them a few hours. They drill holes around the house, inject the insulation and then fill the holes with colour-matched concrete. After a few weeks it's hard to see where they are, but you'll notice the difference in warmth inside immediately.

The cost will be between £200 and £300 on average and you'll get your money back in two years. That's a better return than any savings plan.

Windows

Whatever that ever-so-charming salesman from the double-glazing company might say, the payback in energy savings is not fantastic – but you will improve your comfort level and it is worth doing.

In money your return is likely to be around £140 a year, which means a £3,000 window replacement takes twenty years to recoup. Although I mention a twenty-year payback, don't forget that the new windows may add to the value of your home when selling. My guess – and that's all it can be – is that you add half the cost of the windows to the value of your home, so your payback becomes ten years.

Of course, if your windows need replacing, then it makes sense to install double glazing and to consider specifying coated glass like Pilkington K. The coating reflects heat back into the room while also letting in free heat from the sun.

Check that the windows have the Energy Saving Recommended logo and what rating they are. Just like electric appliances, windows are rated on an A to G scale, A being the best.

Don't bother with secondary glazing. It's not a lot cheaper than new windows, not as efficient as proper double glazing and is a nightmare to keep clean.

Whether you have double or single glazing, don't forget your curtains. Just drawing your curtains at night creates still air between the window and the curtain, so reducing heat loss by convection and cutting out that cold spot. Even better, hang an inner pair of thermal curtain linings and you'll really feel the benefit. That's a much cheaper solution than buying heavy curtains.

Plumbers love to put a radiator under the window. The idea is to pump heat into the coldest part of the room, making it feel warmer and stopping their customer complaining. It's the most inefficient position to place them, but plumbers are a traditional bunch. When you draw the curtains, tuck them behind the radiator and push that heat towards the room, not the window.

In addition to thermal curtains, if you can put a shelf above radiators in front of windows they will really help push the heat back into the room. You need them to be about 200mm (8in) wide.

Controlling the heat

Having stopped the heat loss, the next task is to look at controlling the heat. I have seen someone open a window to cool an overheated room in the depths of winter, dressed in a T-shirt. Then he moaned about the heating bill!

The first thing is to fit a thermostat if your system doesn't have one. Heating systems are at their least efficient in the spring and autumn, when they are needed one day but not the next. An overall thermostat is cheap and will save its cost, including professional fitting, many times over.

Next look at the individual rooms. Radiator thermostatic controls are around £8 each and fairly easy to fit yourself if you're moderately comfortable with plumbing. In theory, on installation of a central heating system, the heating engineer balances the radiators by means of the control valves to bring all the rooms to a preset temperature at the same time. In practice, even if this was done properly, things change. People differ as well; some like a bedroom warm and others prefer it cold, for example.

Thermostatic radiator valves (TRV for short) enable you to precisely control the temperature in each individual room, and you can adjust them for your preference or switch off the radiator in a room not in use. Check the trade plumber's merchants for a price. I got ours for half of what the major DIY discount shed in the town wanted.

While you have the radiators off the wall and the system drained down, fit reflective panels behind them on exterior walls. These are foil-faced foam and just stick to the wall, pushing the heat into the room.

The boiler

Now we've stopped the heat losses and controlled the temperature, we need to consider how we generate it. The vast majority of houses in cities and towns have a piped gas supply. This is the cheapest mass energy source, and it's likely to remain that way for the next twenty years or so.

Old gas boilers (and oil boilers) were pretty unsophisticated and inefficient machines. Over a third – nearly half with some heavy old boilers – of the energy they used to deliver heat to the system just went out of the flue. Modern condensing boilers are almost 90 per cent efficient. So, if you are spending £550 a year heating with an old gas boiler at 55 per cent efficiency, the new condensing one should deliver the same amount of heat to the house where you want it for £355, saving almost £200. Divide the purchase and installation cost by the saving to decide what payback you'll get, usually around five to seven years.

Heat pumps

If your heating fuel is oil, LPG or electricity, then consider a heat-pump system.

The amazing thing about heat-pump systems is that you actually get more energy out of them than you put in. Of course, you never really get something for nothing. Heat-pump systems are comparatively expensive to buy and install, but you can recoup the investment in just three or four years.

They work in a similar way to a fridge, but in reverse. If you feel the fins at the back of your fridge, you'll notice they're warm. What's happening is that the heat from the inside is being pumped to the outside to reduce the temperature in the fridge. A heat-pump system slightly cools the outside world and concentrates the heat in your house, so the energy consumed is being used to pump heat around rather than generate it directly.

From a carbon emission viewpoint, your power source is electricity, but if you sign up to a green tariff where your power is from renewable sources, then you can be very green. Since you're getting far higher efficiency anyway, then even with normal tariffs you're producing less carbon than with an oil-fired or LPG system.

They're really common in Scandinavian countries, where it does get pretty cold, and in heating office buildings in the UK. They're an established, proven technology and the only mystery is that many people don't even seem to have heard of them for domestic heating.

There are three types of heat-pump system, all of which will have an environmental benefit in reducing carbon and realistically recouping your investment in a reasonable time against the fuels mentioned above.

Ground-source heat pump

Here the heat energy is collected by means of pipes buried about 1.2m (4ft) underground. The reason for this is that the temperature at that depth will be fairly stable, winter and summer. That's why mains water pipes are buried, so they don't freeze up in a cold winter.

Obviously this makes an awful mess of a garden during installation (and you need enough space), but it's the most efficient system economically if you can afford the capital outlay. The efficiency is better than air-source heat pumps but the costs are lower than geothermal. If you run the pipes under a black tarmac drive, you improve the system efficiency a little further as the tarmac absorbs warmth from the sun and heats the ground a little.

Do be aware that running the pipes under a vegetable plot is not a good idea as they do slightly cool the ground and, in effect, push spring back a couple of weeks.

Power output is around four times the power input into the system.

Geothermal heat pump

If you are limited in area or can't lay pipes at that depth under the soil, you can drop a deep borehole and run the pipes vertically, usually anything from 30–100m (100–330ft). This is obviously a more specialist – which equals expensive – installation method, but the savings available will very probably make it viable.

The power output against input is comparable with ground-sourced systems.

Air-sourced heat pump

This is the least efficient of the heat-pump systems, typically giving just three times delivered heat to energy input against the 4:1 ratio of the other systems. Still, 300 per cent efficiency is better than 80 per cent with an oil boiler!

The benefit is that these are far cheaper and less disruptive to install and will fit where there is not enough room for the other types of heat pump. Because you have to fit a fan unit outside, rather like a commercial refrigeration system, noise can be a problem, so discussing acoustic insulation with the supplier is a good idea.

They're most efficient in spring and autumn when the air temperature is around 5–12°C (41–54°F), but least efficient in freezing weather. The ground-source systems do benefit from the stable temperature below the soil.

As I said above, it is still well worth replacing an old boiler run on oil or LPG with an air-source pump. If you have storage radiators, then it's a 'no-brainer'.

Woodburners

Wood is a green fuel. Trees take up carbon as they grow and while this is released when it's burnt, as long as another tree is planted and growing in its place, then the overall carbon emissions are basically neutral. Better still, the waste product is wood ash, which is a great potash-rich fertiliser for your garden.

There is something absolutely magical about a log fire or any open fire in the depths of winter; sadly they're very inefficient to run that way. A modern stove, with controlled ventilation, is far more efficient and almost as magical, but is it for you?

Whatever stove you get will require you to clean out the ashes and to feed in new fuel, so they are more work than flicking a switch. It may be fun for a short while, but it can become yet another chore which is something to consider. Having said that, I've not tired of playing with our woodburner after six years.

Where are you going to get your fuel? If you happen to own a three-acre wood, then you would be silly to look at any other fuel. Most of us, though, don't have easy access to bulk supplies of wood.

Of course, you can buy logs to burn, seasoned (which just means dried) hard or softwood, but this is quite expensive. Some joinery companies and mills will supply scrap wood offcuts and logs made by compressing sawdust at reasonable cost. A lot depends on how far you are from them. If you have to drive many miles then it doesn't make economic or ecological sense to use the petrol driving back and forth.

We burn quite a lot of old pallets. Chopping up the flat pieces produces great kindling sticks. **Tip** I wear a chainsaw glove on my left hand and use the hand axe with the right when making kindling sticks. It's saved me from a really nasty injury a couple of times.

If you're burning scrap wood or old pallets, don't worry about removing nails and screws. Obviously you don't want them in the ashes when you use them on the garden, so just trail a magnet through the ashes and fish out the nails. Easy!

Don't forget that you'll need somewhere to cut and store your wood. You can't use recently cut logs as they'll be too wet. Usually freshly chopped logs need to be dried for a year to bring the moisture content down below 20 per cent. They can take up a fair amount of space, so not ideal for small gardens.

You need to check with your local authority if you are in a designated smoke control area under the Clean Air Act 1993. If so, this will affect the type of stove you can get. Generally, the more efficient stoves comply with legislation.

There's a huge range of stoves available, from those designed to heat just a room to those with a boiler to run a house-heating system, and prices range from a couple of hundred pounds to thousands. There's even a woodburner with an automatic temperature control and a remote-control unit, if you win the lottery. At one time you could pick up stoves cheaply second-hand but nowadays that's not so easy. As with any appliance, shop around.

Don't forget you'll need a fireproof plate to sit the stove on and nine times out of ten you'll need to have a flue liner fitted because the stoves are efficient. The gasses are cool compared with those from old coal fires and tars can condense in the chimney, which can then build up and catch fire.

When buying a woodburning stove, ask about efficiency. Some of the latest stoves are extremely efficient which means you'll use less wood. It's worth considering what size of log will fit in, as chopping logs into small lengths is time-consuming.

Although woodburners aren't usually difficult to install, there are rules to follow regarding ventilation and safety. Legally the installation should be certificated, which in practice means using a HETAS approved installer (see www.hetas.co.uk).

You will need a carbon monoxide alarm, and a stove thermometer that measures chimney temperature is a good idea for efficient control. One accessory that we found brilliant was a stovetop fan, powered by the heat of the stove. It distributes the heat around the room and makes a huge difference on a cold day.

In conclusion, woodburning stoves are wonderful if you have a cheap and plentiful source of wood, but not so much otherwise. Like other biofuels, growing trees for fuel on land unsuitable for food production could make a valuable contribution to our national energy needs, but it's not a solution for everyone – if only because we don't have enough land.

Biomass boilers

These are designed to heat the whole house and water supply just like gas or oil boilers. Usually they use wood pellets made from specially grown willow trees, but some run on logs. There are various models and different levels of automation. Some are fed automatically and the ash is also removed automatically. They're not a cheap installation – £5,000 is not uncommon – but worth looking at, especially as the prices are still falling and there may be government incentives. It's also worth checking if there's a wood fuel co-operative in your area, such as the Dartmoor Wood Fuel Co-operative in Devon.

Government financial incentives

At the time of writing, the government is offering incentives to encourage people to install renewable energy generation and for heat pumps and biomass heating. However, the rates offered are subject to change and there is no guarantee that they will continue. Before installing a new heating system or replacing an older one, check what is available. The best website for clear, unbiased information is the Energy Saving Trust: www.energysavingtrust.org.uk

Generating your own power

The concept of solar power or wind power is very seductive; we all like getting something for nothing. Sadly it doesn't quite work like that in reality.

Wind generators

I love wind generators. If you go to Tarifa in southern Spain where the wind sweeps in from the Strait of Gibraltar, the mountaintops are crowned with row upon row of majestically turning wind turbines. A truly awesome sight.

However, at the domestic scale it's greenwash madness. There is no way that you will ever get your investment back. The generator will have worn out long before you've a reasonable prospect of that. Worse still, one study concluded that the energy produced in a small wind generator's lifetime would not compensate for the carbon emissions created in its manufacture.

The commercial large-scale generators are carefully sited in places where they'll get a fairly consistent flow of wind, hence the offshore developments. A small wind generator that is fixed to the average house will suffer turbulence and probably only run at 30 per cent of its rating at best.

If you want to build your own wind generator – on the same basis as some men like to build steam engines – then fine. But don't be kidded that it will save you money or benefit the environment.

Solar power

The technology for photovoltaic electricity-generating solar panels has improved a lot in recent years and it's still developing. They're becoming more and more efficient and the price is still falling.

However, there are still some problems with solar electricity generation. The power is only produced in the day, even if they now generate on cloudy days as well as sunny ones. Many people are out in the day and most household electricity is used at night.

Ideally you would store the electricity made in the day in a battery and use it at night, but the technology isn't quite there yet. We need a battery that will last for twenty years or more, compact, with high capacity and cheap. There are some promising technologies in the labs but nothing on the market that quite fits the bill yet.

The government kick-started the solar-panel business in the UK by the introduction of feed-in tariffs. The surplus power is fed back into the grid and the producer is paid a rate. Initially the rate was very generous, perhaps too generous, but now they've been drastically reduced. My advice is to check the rates on offer and do your sums carefully to calculate payback time. Currently it's around twenty-five years which isn't very attractive, but if the price of an installation halves, it would be well worth having if you have spare cash to invest.

Don't forget that the panel's efficiency will fall over the years and while they should last twenty years or more, the inverter that converts their 12V output to 230V AC (like mains power) is unlikely to last more than ten years. However, in ten years the price for an inverter will most likely have halved and its efficiency increased.

One consequence of the feed-in tariff system has been the construction of solar farms where fields have been covered in panels. Not only are they pretty unsightly, they also take agricultural land out of production. It would be far more sensible to install panels on the roofs of industrial units and factories. They're no more unsightly than the buildings they sit on and the power could be directly used to offset the factory's consumption, which takes place in the day.

Aside from powering the house, I rather like the kits you can buy designed to power a shed light or a fishpond fountain. They make a lot of sense since running a mains supply up the garden can be an expensive business.

I also rather like recharging our rechargeable batteries with solar power. The kit didn't cost any more than a mains battery charger and it's magical getting 'free power'.

One obvious use for solar technology is water heating. Despite our notorious lack of sunshine, I've experienced hot water coming from a demonstration unit on a cold winter's day with sleet falling at the Centre for Alternative Technology in Machynlleth in mid-Wales.

You don't try to supply all your hot water needs with panels. What you do is to pre heat your water so your main boiler has less work to do to supply hot water. This usually involves an additional water tank being installed, but it gets tricky if you have a combi boiler which is designed to heat mains-pressure water.

You need a southerly facing, unshaded roof to install the panels on and you probably should check with your local authority if any planning permissions are required. There are now a large number of companies offering installed solar water-heating systems, but the problem is cost. There are two main types of panel: flat plate and the more efficient evacuated tube systems. In cost terms you can expect to pay anything from £2,000 to £4,000 for flat plate and up to £6,000 for an evacuated tube installation. However, your hot water is unlikely to be costing you much above £150 a year to produce so the payback is not very attractive at anything from fifteen years to thirty years.

If you have some plumbing and building skills then it's quite possible to build your own solar panels using recycled old radiators as panels. The exact 'how to do it' is the subject of a book in itself, but you could get the cost down to around £500 if you have the necessary skills. At this point the economics really make sense. From an environmental point of view, fitting solar panels makes sense, but economically it has to be a DIY job.

Space heating

The other sensible use for solar power is space heating and, surprisingly, cooling. If you've got a conservatory on your house, you've probably noticed it can get stiflingly hot very quickly when the sun shines, even when it's cold outside.

The hottest air collects in the apex of the conservatory roof, so running an air vent through to the house is a very simple way to collect free hot air. Obviously you need to open and close a vent – you don't want it running at night – but it's simple and surprisingly effective.

In the summer you can even reverse the process by leaving a door from the house open to the conservatory and having an opening light in the conservatory roof. As the air heats in the conservatory, it rises and escapes through the roof creating a cooling breeze in the house as air flows into the conservatory to replace it.

This may sound a bit 'Heath Robinson' but it's based on sound principles that have been incorporated into many buildings and used as a cooling system for low-impact housing in Arizona. The idea was patented back in 1881 by an American inventor named Edward Morse, but the concept was properly developed by French engineer Felix Trombe in 1964 who developed the Trombe Wall for a house based on passive solar heating in France.

One surprising use for Trombe Walls is in cooling houses in hot areas rather than using air conditioning. The idea is to use the rising heat to generate a cooling breeze through the house.

It's surprising that these passive solar heating and cooling concepts are not better known or more popular. Building houses as we do in Britain with no consideration of the potential benefits of solar power is a disgrace. We could save huge amounts of energy by just building our houses with large windows on the south side to catch the sun and small on the north to minimise loss.

Building in solar panels as a replacement for roof tiles, solar space heating conservatories or greenhouses as standard and high insulation levels would recoup the relatively small additional cost many times over in the building's life. Retro-fitting is inevitably more expensive and far less likely to actually happen.

An energy audit

Have you ever looked at your electricity bill and wondered how on earth it got to that? It's well worth taking a long hard look at what electricity you use and performing an energy audit. We invested in a device that measures how much power has been consumed over time. It cost only £7 but has more than saved that by showing us where and how much electricity things use.

Just go into each room in your house with pencil and paper and make notes. You'll be surprised.

Start at the top: the light bulb (I hope it's a low-energy one). The latest technology for lighting is LED, which is quickly replacing the compact fluorescent lights that replaced the old incandescent bulbs. Unlike the compact fluorescents, which often took a while to warm up, LED lights are instantly on. Theoretically they should eventually offer a lifespan of 100,000 hours, but currently they offer 20 to 30,000 hours' life. This is due to the electronics that transform mains power down to the LEDs. It's a developing technology.

Avoid the very cheap bulbs available on eBay. The quality is often very poor and the life very short. I'm told this is due to the electronics being built for 230V systems and our power nominally 240V but actually peaking to 250V at times. Whatever the reason, our experiences with cheap LED bulbs have been very disappointing. Bulbs purchased from major retailers are far more reliable.

It's well worth replacing halogen lights with LED. Halogen lights claim to be low energy but that is in comparison with the old-fashioned incandescent bulbs. LED replacements use approximately a tenth of the power of halogen. There is one thing to watch out for, though. Mains-powered halogens are easily replaced, but 12V systems can be a problem. These use a transformer which outputs 12V AC, whereas LEDs use a driver that outputs 12V DC. Sometimes they're fine, but you may find the bulbs flickering madly with a transformer. Happily, changing the transformer for an LED driver is not expensive and usually easy. If you're not sure, as with all electrical work, call a professional.

Don't forget the best costcutter with lighting is the off switch. Despite what you may have heard about it being more efficient to leave fluorescents on, the truth is that as long as the light is off for more than 9 seconds, switching off is better.

In our kitchen we've a gas cooker with a built-in clock. It only uses 5 watts. That's 46 units a year or £5.50. Then there's the telephone. It's a walk-around model sitting on a charger and that costs us about the same as the clock. It's ironic to think that I was pleased to buy the phone on sale and save £10, never thinking about the electricity it uses. Old-fashioned fixed phones are powered from the phone system and cost nothing to run except the call costs.

Next there's the radio. That's got a little clock – why, I don't know – and another fiver goes onto the bill. This is before we look at running any of the appliances.

Move into the lounge and it gets even worse. Here we have the dreaded standby. There was a time when we had adverts on the television reminding us to unplug the TV before we went to bed. Now we just spend half an hour searching out an array of remote controls from the back of the sofa to press the standby button. There's the TV, DVD, Freeview box, video, satellite and the stereo. Why we need a clock on the stereo, that even says goodbye when we put it on standby, is beyond me.

If we could switch them all off properly we'd save over £30 a year on those alone. You can actually buy a remote-controlled plug socket which switches off the appliances that have remote controls. Or you can bend over and flick a switch on the socket for free.

It doesn't stop there; you switch off your computer, the monitor goes blank and that should be it, but it's not of course. The monitor is in sleep mode, quietly drawing a few watts, and even the computer isn't properly off. There's a little light saying it's still drawing power. Then there's the printer and the scanner: they're still drawing some energy. We now have them all on one extension cable with multiple outlets and one flick of the switch kills the lot. **Tip** Always turn your computer off with the system control before switching the power off, or you can damage the software.

Some estimates state that 25 per cent of our electricity bill is made up of these unnoticed appliances, quietly sitting in the background eating away. The question is, 'Do you want to throw money away, or manually flick a switch?'

Appliances

If you're buying a new appliance, whether it be a fridge or a washing machine, you'll find that it is rated as to its energy efficiency: A rated is the best and G the worst. As a general rule, if you can't pick up a decent second-hand appliance, it's worth paying a bit more for the A rated. It's easy to forget the energy rating when you look at the array of features and designs of modern appliances, but you'll pay for that inattention for years to come.

Incidentally, don't bother with those extended warranties the retailers love to sell you with anything electrical. You have a legal right to a guarantee for at least the first year and the insurers know that if the appliances work out of the box, then they're most likely to keep running for five years anyway so the retailers are on a very safe bet extending the warranty for a couple of years. When the appliance dies – and all machines do – the chances are the replacement will be better and cheaper anyway.

If you feel more comfortable with an extended warranty, it's usually worth buying them separately rather than from the retailer.

Washing machines

Modern washing machines are getting to be very efficient and can be awfully clever; some are too clever for their own good, even assessing a suitable wash program and temperature. If you're buying a new one, go for the simplest you can find and preferably one with a separate temperature control. Not just because there is less to go wrong but because it puts you in control. Washing at 30°C is less than half the cost of 60°C.

We measured the difference between a quick and cool wash (with an extra spin to dry the clothes more) with a full 60°C wash. One was 7p and the other 20p at an electricity cost of 11.7p per unit. If you have a baby in the house, then you know how much you use the washing machine and can see how the costs can really mount up.

Tumble dryers

Yes, they're expensive to run and they're hardly green but when it's been raining for a week and the baby's clothes need drying, what can you do? Actually, there are things you can do. Try a clothes horse, which is just a rack you pop up in a room and hang the washing on. You can get handy racks that hook on a radiator, so you're using the heat already in the house. They can cause damp air and condensation problems, though.

It's well worth putting the washing machine on an extra spin cycle before you take your washing out. It hardly uses any energy to spin again and it does cut down the drying time.

If you have to use a dryer, then consider getting some Dryerballs® – these are special balls that heat up in the tumble dryer and reduce the drying time by a quarter. They also seem to act like a fabric softener, which is a nice bonus.

Dishwashers

We're a bit strange about dishwashers in Britain. Nearly every family has a washing machine and sees nothing wrong with it, but dishwashers are considered almost sinful. Perhaps it's because we had to take our turn at the washing up as children – and woe betide us if we didn't – or maybe it was the sign of a slovenly person being too lazy to wash up immediately after a meal.

Whatever, the truth is that a dishwasher, used correctly, uses less water and energy than hand washing and is more hygienic. By 'used correctly' I mean by following a few simple rules. Rinse off any plates with cold water before loading, and if a plate just has a few crumbs from a sandwich don't bother putting it in. Rinse with cold water and leave in the rack. Perfectly clean, no energy use and just a little water. The same goes with pans used for boiling some vegetables. They're not dirty and a quick rinse is all they need.

Don't use the dishwasher half full. It uses the same water, energy and powder as when full. Instead put it through a rinse cycle, which uses a little cold water, and leave it with the door shut until the next day when you continue loading. When it is full, use the lowest wash cycle you can. Our machine has a 35°C quick wash which is perfectly sufficient 90 per cent of the time.

So if you've always wanted a dishwasher but felt it too sinful to have one, now you can. Just tell everyone it's the green option!

Fridges and freezers

Our freezers are an important part of our low-cost living strategy. We store our own home-grown vegetables, batch-cooked meals and supermarket bargains. In fact we have three freezers for the two of us!

It's a sad fact that well over half of the fridges (and probably a similar proportion of freezers) that end up on the tip actually work perfectly well, which is why you can usually pick up a second-hand freezer for peanuts in your local paper. The saving you make on the buying price more than makes up for them not being quite as efficient as a new model.

Chest freezers usually have the lowest price for capacity when buying new, and the running costs are pretty low. Avoid the 'frost-free' machines. It doesn't take long to defrost a freezer manually every six months or so, and the frost-free machines cost a lot more to run.

Fridge-freezers and freezers come with a star rating in addition to the energy efficiency rating. Four stars means that the freezer will reach -18°C (-0.4°F) or colder and is capable of freezing fresh foods. Three stars means that the freezer runs at -18°C but is not able to freeze fresh food. Ensure your freezer is four star, since being able to freeze your own produce and supermarket bargains is vital for low-cost living.

When buying a freezer, check how long it will hold temperature in the event of a power cut. This can be as little as 8 hours or as long as 36 hours. Living as we do now in the countryside, power cuts are not unknown, so holding temperature is important to us.

CHAPTER EIGHTEEN

Water

We're fortunate to live in a country where, nine years out of ten, the summer resembles a monsoon season and water falls from the sky. Yet in that tenth year, when we find ourselves basking in the sunshine, there's a drought.

This is inevitably accompanied by the water companies' demands that we save water, hosepipe bans and threats of fines for watering the garden (despite the fact that they lose millions of litres through leaking pipes they deem uneconomical to repair).

The big problem with water in the UK is that the western and northern areas get the lion's share of the rainfall, but our population is concentrated in London and the south-east. Water is often extracted from rivers and that's causing serious problems in some places as we're extracting so much that the water flow is reduced. This causes the river to silt up, killing the fish and destroying the ecology of adjacent areas.

One answer would be to create a national water grid (as we have for electricity), taking water from the wet areas to the dry. This would involve new reservoirs flooding valleys and hundreds of miles of high-volume pipes across the country at an astronomical cost and scars across the landscape.

Perhaps a more sensible approach – at least in the water-short areas of the country – would be to build new houses designed to use less water and subsidise water-saving measures for existing housing stock.

The water we use has all been purified to a high standard and is safely drinkable, but then we go and use it to flush our toilets, wash the car and water the garden. This highlights an easy way to reduce that water usage and thereby improve the environment. Collect and use rainwater that falls onto the roof and currently goes directly to the sewer system. Our first house, built in 1938, had a galvanised tank on the flat roof above the kitchen which was fed from the guttering and supplied a special tap in the kitchen to provide soft water for washing.

It would be fairly straightforward and inexpensive to build in a rainwater tank and plumb it to feed the toilets in a new house, although retro-fitting to an existing house would be more expensive. It would also need a feed from the mains to the tank to cope with dry periods.

Even with all that the potential saving isn't huge – in the order of 50 litres a day or 18 cubic metres per year for the average family against the 130 cubic metres used. Still, even a 10 per cent reduction would have a large environmental impact.

You can make very significant, cost-effective savings by tapping into your guttering to fill a water butt or two. All you need is a diverter and filter that fixes into the downpipe, which will set you back about £6, and tanks to store the water.

The tankage is where the money can come in. Old plastic barrels as water butts can often be found for free, but you can find purpose-made water butts quite cheaply. Check if your water company is offering any subsidised deals. Water butts come in different sizes and prices but if you have room for a large tank, look for an IBC water tank on eBay. These tanks hold 1,000 litres in a plastic tank held in a metal cage. You can even stack one on top of another. Add in a small on-demand pump and you'll be able to use a hosepipe in the garden. Hosepipe bans don't apply to your own saved water, so no problem with piping your water to the plants even if there's a ban. The plants generally prefer rainwater to treated tap water, so that's another benefit.

In a drought, water at dusk or at night so that the hot sun of the day doesn't cause it to just evaporate. Soaker or leaky hoses are a very efficient way to deliver water directly to crops in borders, but sprinklers use huge amounts of water and are not. It's better to water thoroughly once every few days rather than just put on a little as the moisture will stay on the surface and actually encourages shallow root development.

Do keep water butts covered to keep out wildlife and inquisitive children. One great tip for keeping the water sweet is to add a few crystals of potassium permanganate (obtainable from the chemist) or even a drop or two of vinegar.

Incidentally, using rainwater to supply all the household needs is feasible in the wetter areas of the country. Our neighbours are off-grid and all their water arrives from the roof. However, purifying it to drinking standard isn't cheap. It requires storage, pump, special filters and UV sterilisation with expensive bulbs that have to be replaced frequently. They reckon that mains water is a bargain!

There are other things you can do to reduce your water usage. It's possible to reduce your consumption by a quarter without too much effort.

- **Turn off the tap** while brushing your teeth. It won't save a fortune, but every little helps.
- **When replacing taps**, fit spray taps that introduce air into the flow. They save quite a bit and seem to make washing more effective.
- **Consider showering** instead of taking a bath. A shower generally uses less than half the 80 litres of water used in a bath.
- **Always use dishwashers and washing machines** when full. If you're buying a new machine, go for an energy- and water-efficient model.
- **With toilets**, use a water displacement device to cut the water used in every flush, or get a new dual-flush or low-flush model when replacing.
- **Always mend dripping taps promptly** – they waste far more water than you might imagine.

Reducing your water bill

Homes built after 1990 have a water meter fitted, so reducing your use will have an immediate effect on the bills. If you've an older property you can have a water meter fitted but be careful. Without a meter, your bill is based on the rateable value of the house rather than usage. If, as a family, you use a lot of water you can end up with higher bills.

There is an out, though: you can switch back to the rateable value system if you make the request to do so within twelve months of having the water meter installed. So if you've made a mistake and you're going to be paying more, there is a way out.

If you are on a meter and have a low income, or an occupant in your house who needs to use a lot of water, check with your supplier about the low WaterSure tariff. Single-person households can get a fixed tariff, which is another potential money-saver.

Your water bill actually covers three things: the water you use, sewerage and rain that falls on the roof that goes down the drain. If your rainwater drains into a soakaway on your property you may be entitled to a reduction on your charges. Ask your water supplier.

If your sewerage goes into a septic tank then you should not be paying for sewerage with your water bill. It's worth checking your bill is only for water supply.

CHAPTER NINETEEN

Transport

We live in a society where coping without a car is almost impossible.

Corner shops are almost a thing of the past, and many villages no longer even have one. Public transport has become a rare sight in many parts of the country. Of course our large cities are well catered for – buses, metro links and Underground services – but move into a village with one bus a day (if you are lucky) and you'll need a car. Even many towns no longer have a centre; the shops are out of town on soulless estates isolated (except by road) from the community they 'serve'.

When I was a child, bus stops were thronged with children making their way to school and adults on their way to work. Now we see droves of under-occupied people carriers doing the school run so their offspring have no further to walk than a few yards from roadside to school gate. Then the driver heads off to the out-of-town superstore to fill the day until it is time to pick up the children from school.

But unless and until we return to frequent and convenient public transport, the car is going to be the mainstay for us, and that is going to mean oil as the main fuel for years to come.

I don't believe oil will suddenly run out; there are vast reserves that are uneconomical to extract until the price consistently rises. Make no mistake, it will rise inexorably year after year. I remember the fuss when it hit £1 a gallon and it recently went over £1 a litre – that's about £5 a gallon. Five pounds a litre will be the next milestone – and it may be sooner than we expect.

The car industry is a huge employer, and one which the government doesn't want to fail and thereby put too many people out of work. On the other hand, they want to cut down our level of carbon emissions, and transport is largely responsible for this. So rather than put a real investment into public transport, we have the myth of the green car.

There's no such thing as a 'green car'

There are some cars that are less damaging to the environment than others, some that produce less CO_2 than others, but no car is green (except for the paint colour).

First of all, every car has to be manufactured. Even the greenest car will use metals, plastics and produce huge amounts of waste in the process of mining, refining and shipping those metals to the factory gate. That's before they're shaped, welded and put together with thousands of other components and shipped to the local dealer.

Once that car is made, it starts down the road to the scrapyard, where yet more energy is going to be expended in tearing it apart and crushing the remains.

There is a myth that electric cars are non-polluting, and they certainly don't produce exhaust fumes. But they do have batteries and these do not last for ever, although great efforts are being made to increase their storage capacity and lifespan. Once their life is over they also have to be disposed of.

Electricity has to be generated and renewable sources are still only a small proportion of that, so effectively you are still using a fossil fuel. The pollution has been 'pushed away' from the end user, but it still exists.

There's been a lot of talk about biofuels and running cars on old chip fat. It's a wonderful idea, but growing crops for biofuels displaces food crops and leads to shortages and hunger. There just isn't enough old chip fat to go round, either. It makes for good TV but it's not a real solution for the masses.

So having accepted that you cannot get a green car, the question becomes:

What car does the least harm?

Bearing in mind a huge amount of energy goes into manufacturing a car, running a less-efficient older model is probably greener than buying a new one.

Economically it rarely pays to buy a new car. Most of the depreciation happens as you drive off the forecourt but, as the manufacturers get desperate for sales, some new car deals can make it worthwhile.

Obviously go for the car with the least emissions, if only to keep the tax down, and small is beautiful. There's not really any point in having a car that does 0 to 60mph in 4 seconds with a top speed of 160mph on British roads where the average speed in cities is now lower than in the days of horse-drawn carts.

If you do a lot of long-distance driving, then you know a larger car is better. That extra bit of space, slightly better acceleration and so on does make a difference. However, if you look at where you actually drive, you may be surprised. Most of your journeys will be relatively short, perhaps less than 5 miles, with just the occasional long journey.

When we downsized our car, for a week or two it did feel a little cramped. After that we didn't notice that it was smaller. We did notice the lower bills, filling up less often and for less money. Our car tax each year fell away, as did the insurance cost. That we noticed with a smile. And it did fit into tight parking spaces easily.

Is your journey really necessary?

Whatever car you drive, you can cut down your car usage. For a start, many families have two cars and neither of them is used to the full. When you look at the total cost of a car, it's frightening. Many families can adjust to one car quite easily with minimal inconvenience. For example, in a two-car family often one partner takes the children to school and then goes on to work while the other goes straight to work where the car sits until it is time to return home. At the weekend, one car isn't used at all. By leaving earlier and one partner dropping the other off, that additional cost can be removed.

Of course it is less convenient if one partner has to be dropped off and picked up from work, but on the plus side maybe you both won't need to work so hard when you don't have to pay for the depreciation, repairs, insurance and tax on your underused car.

Even if it isn't possible for one to drop the other off and there's no reasonable public transport, consider using a taxi. If you have a regular run, it's worth asking the driver about a discount. It may cost more than the petrol, but don't forget those other 'hidden' costs.

Perhaps there is a workmate – or maybe two or three – who live near to you and with whom you could car share. You'll need to contribute to the costs but you are saving your depreciation, insurance, tax, maintenance and fuel costs. Not to mention the parking problems when you get to work. As a general rule this won't affect your car insurance, but you should check with your insurance company as policies do vary between firms.

Many people drive surprisingly short distances, so try walking instead. It's a good way to keep fit and far less stressful than screaming at the car in front to get out of the way. Don't forget that on foot you can nip up alleyways and go the wrong way up one-way streets. Your journey might even be faster than using the car in some towns.

Do you actually need to make the journey? It's surprising how often we nip out to the shop for something we may need, but not that day. Think ahead and plan your journey efficiently so you don't double back on yourself. Not only do you save money, you save time as well.

How to reduce your fuel consumption

If you must drive, then there are ways you can significantly and easily reduce your fuel consumption. The first thing is to keep your car in good condition and regularly serviced. You need to be safe anyway, and an engine failure in the fast lane on the motorway is nearly as dangerous as brake failure. Make sure you top up with the correct grade of engine oil and that your tyres are in good condition and correctly inflated. Under-inflated tyres create more drag on the road and you can easily save 5 per cent off your fuel bill by pumping them up. Don't forget that you may need a higher pressure if you have a heavy load. The manufacturer's handbook will give you the correct levels.

There was a time when no car owner would dream of going on a long journey without checking water, oil and tyres. The reliability of modern cars has made us complacent, but you could be paying for it.

Don't carry extra weight if you don't need to. If the boot is full of things, clean it out. You know you're going to have to do it one day, so do it now. Roof racks can be useful but they create a lot of drag and increase fuel consumption, so take them off when you don't need them.

The way you drive is where the big savings come in. Drive like granny on a bad day and you'll see what I mean. Smooth acceleration and deceleration, changing up a gear earlier rather than later will make a huge difference. After all, it's a road not a racetrack. I'm always amused to see the car in front race off and then screech to a halt at the next set of traffic lights, as I calmly coast up behind him. It doesn't just save you money, it's a lot less stressful and safer.

Speed limits indicate a maximum speed, not a minimum. The Department for Transport states that driving at 70mph uses up to 9 per cent more fuel than at 60mph, and up to 15 per cent more than at 50mph. Cruising at 80mph can use up to 25 per cent more fuel than at 70mph. That's a huge difference for very little time saving even if you don't get caught!

There is nothing shameful about being in the inside lane on the motorway. In fact, with all the hold-ups on our road system, I've found that it is often quicker to stick behind a lorry. They're expert drivers and it's often a case of the tortoise beating the hare.

Modern cars have sophisticated fuel-management systems, so there is no point in coasting with the engine off (always a dangerous thing to do anyway). However, there are a few more things you can do to reduce your fuel consumption further.

- **In cold weather**, don't sit waiting for the car to warm up before starting off. Cars warm up faster when driving and it's very wasteful. In fact, if you're stuck in a jam for more than a minute it will pay you to switch off the engine and restart when the traffic moves again. Always keep your eyes on the car in front of the one in front so you don't get hooted at by the impatient chap behind when they move.

- **As soon as the car has warmed up**, switch off screen heaters and reduce the blower speed. Electrical consumption uses fuel and every bit helps.
- **In a hot summer**, air conditioning is a real luxury but it drinks fuel. As soon as the car is cooled down and tolerable, switch it off. Open the windows a small amount and turn up the blowers. Driving with the window fully open increases drag and fuel consumption, so avoid that if you can.
- **It's well worth measuring your fuel consumption**, if only to reinforce the good driving habits you are developing. Fill the car up and make a note of the mileage, then drive around until your tank is half or more used. Then go back to the same pump at the same garage and fill up again. Try to go back to the same pump to ensure a level playing field; another pump might be on a slope and affect the reading. Now, note your new mileage and how many litres of fuel you've used. This used to be an easier calculation before metrification, but that's what we have calculators for! Divide the total miles driven in the period by the number of litres of fuel used and then multiply by 4.546 to convert to miles per gallon. It's well worth repeating on occasion, just to check bad habits aren't creeping in and you're not starting to confuse your car with an F1 racecar again.
- **Don't forget to keep your eye out for the cheapest petrol supplier** in your area.

Shop around for insurance

Purely on the subject of running costs, you can probably save a lot on your insurance. I don't know why, but when they send a renewal quote it's often astronomical. You shop around and find the best price, but a year later they seem to think your brains have evaporated. We've actually had a quote from our insurance company as a new customer for £150 less than they wanted on the renewal notice to us as an existing customer. I'm sure it makes sense to someone.

Incidentally, this shopping around also makes sense on home insurance. I'm sure they rely on us not bothering to check and just ticking the renewal box each year. Keep swapping companies each year until one of them wakes up and offers a good deal every time you need to renew.

Other forms of transport

Motorbikes and mopeds

I suppose a lot of the drawbacks with cars apply to motorbikes and mopeds. They use fossil fuels, need insuring, taxing and servicing and so on, but they are certainly far greener and cheaper than a car.

Strangely the smaller two-stroke 50cc scooters only achieve around 70mpg, whereas the larger 125cc four-stroke machines get around 80mpg. Still, that's better than most cars – and they're cheaper to buy.

For one person they make good sense for commuting but they do have one major problem: you have to share the road with cars and lorries. Most car drivers are just not aware of bikes. They crowd them too closely, cut across them at junctions and often don't seem to realise that they have a right to be on the road. Lorries and buses are, in my experience, worse if anything.

A good biker friend of mine explained how motorbikes are just as safe as cars so long as the rider keeps his wits about him. He was in hospital at the time as a car had pulled out from a junction into him, so I'm not so sure.

Bicycles

I've mixed feelings about bicycles as well. They're cheap to buy, often available second-hand and fairly easy to maintain yourself. In terms of speed, they're not bad either. A normal, unfit person will get 10mph on the flat without getting exhausted. I've heard cyclists in London talk about getting 15mph on their way to work, twice the average 7mph the rush-hour traffic achieves in the city.

Certainly bicycles are very green, using zero fuel and having a low manufacturing cost, and of course they help keep you fit. However, the same safety concerns as for motorbikes apply. Economically and ecologically they are brilliant but, from a safety point of view, they're not so good. Most cycling accidents happen in urban areas, so you're probably safer in the country (although there are issues with narrow lanes and tourist drivers etc). Hopefully the increase in cycle lanes will make the bicycle a safer proposition.

The other problem with push bikes is they tend not to get used much after people have bought them. As I said, they're great on the flat but, when you have steep hills to get up, the bicycle loses some appeal unless you're really fit.

There is a good option though: the electric bicycle. Since the motor is used more to supplement your efforts than replace them, you still get some exercise and fresh air but you're not going to end up sweating and trembling if there is a hill to negotiate. In terms of energy, they're very cheap to charge. I've seen figures suggesting they give the equivalent of 800 to 2,000mpg (converting electricity to the equivalent in petrol).

Because they are less effort than a pushbike – but still have the advantages – the fact is an electric bike owner is far more likely to actually use it. They have to be worth looking at, at least.

There's one final point in favour of the bicycle. There is a scheme whereby employers can offer them to workers on a subsidised basis. This applies to electric bikes as well. Check out www.cyclescheme.co.uk.

Trains and coaches

If you're going on a long journey, then do consider coach or train. Trains, despite what you may think, tend to be reliable – more reliable than cars or coaches, which get stuck in traffic. But coaches are often cheaper, which is a shame since well-occupied trains are greener. The Internet is a real boon here. So long as you plan a few weeks ahead, you can often get fares quite cheaply. The nearer to your journey day, the more expensive it gets.

A journey from our home in Cheshire to central London would be around 170 miles, which the AA estimate would cost about £93.50 each way, so that's £187 in total. On top of that there's the congestion charge of £11.50 (and I dread to think how much the parking would cost). Don't forget your car costs include servicing, depreciation and so forth as well as fuel. Admittedly, if we ignore the standing charges the running costs are less.

The same journey by train, booked in advance (off-peak) was just £34. Add to that taxi and Tube fares of around £20. Don't forget: the journey will take an hour and a half less, all things being equal, and is far less stressful. You can't read a book and drive a car at the same time.

A similar journey by coach could save even more but takes about an hour longer than by car. It all depends on how much of a rush you are in.

CHAPTER TWENTY

Recycling

The huge rubbish dump landfills are filling up and it's become a major problem. Nobody wants to live next to an incinerator, and who can blame them? You only have to look at our bins to see why. At one time a waist-high bin was collected each week by the binmen and carried to the lorry. Now our refuse disposal operatives manoeuvre bulging wheelie bins to huge compacting lorries where they are lifted by machines, being too heavy for a person. Some houses even have extra-large wheelie bins.

On top of this 'rubbish' bin we have boxes or additional bins for our recyclable waste which has to be sorted into the correct box or bin.

In an effort to reduce waste going to the landfill, rubbish-bin collection has moved to fortnightly (and even four-weekly) in some counties. Hearing some people moaning about this quite annoys me, to be frank. Most of the moaners don't bother with the recycling bins, just bunging anything unwanted into that rubbish bin.

I have to wonder how they would have coped in World War II with those wartime regulations. For example, during the war it was an offence to burn or destroy waste paper and cardboard or to mix it with general refuse. Punishment ranged from a fine of £100 (over £4,000 in today's money) to two years' imprisonment.

Those recycle bins and boxes are collected and then taken to central points where they are re-sorted. In fairness, it's often not very clear exactly which plastics are recyclable, but in some Scandinavian countries they have an efficient system where a deposit is charged on plastic bottles. They're taken back to the store and passed into a hole where a machine reads the barcode, sorts them and issues a deposit refund ticket.

The real problem with plastic waste is the huge volume, and particularly the damage it is doing to the marine environment. Thousands of marine species, including sea turtles and whales, are harmed, and hundreds of millions of creatures killed outright by plastic waste.

We need to stop polluting and clean up the mess before it is too late and our children's children inherit a devastated environment. As individuals we can all try to minimise our use of plastics and dispose of our waste responsibly.

Cut down on waste – give your rubbish a second life

Food and garden waste are fairly easy to cut out of the bin. Avoid making the food waste and compost your green waste. The big problem is the mass of packaging much of the food arrives in. Foamed plastic trays wrapped in cling film are the norm for all sorts of things from fruit to meat. If you can buy alternatives with less unnecessary packaging, do so. Empty margarine cartons have another life as home freezer packs, as do those plastic boxes the occasional Chinese takeaway comes in. Empty 4-pint plastic milk bottles are filled with sand or water and used as bricks on the vegetable plot to hold down horticultural fleece. It's surprising the uses you can find for rubbish.

When you make your own wine, ask the neighbours for their old bottles – never mind taking them off to the bottle bank! And glass jars are precious, especially the ones that come with a coated lid suitable for use with chutneys. (The bare metal lids react badly with the vinegar: see Chapter 7.)

Like many people, we use a shredder to avoid confidential information like bank statements being stolen for identity theft. In fact, you can shred any paper and it will compost down. Newspapers don't need shredding as such; just tear them up before composting. The only paper we put into the recycle bin is the glossy magazine stuff and leaflets that always come through the door. Cardboard has its uses as well. It insulates the sides of our compost bins, acts as a weed-suppressing mat for garden paths and eventually rots down to join the soil.

Some things are best left to the professional recyclers – tin cans being one, and plastic bottles that we can't find another use for – but by reducing the input and reusing where we can, I think we've halved the amount that gets taken away in all those bins and boxes each week.

It doesn't stop there, though. A lot of things we no longer need are perfectly serviceable and probably of use to someone. The rise of eBay, where you can easily buy and sell to a global market, means that your 'rubbish' can actually have another life – and make you a little money.

If the money isn't important – and, let's face it, it can be a lot of trouble for little return selling via an Internet auction – then why not give it away on Freecycle? The idea is that people in your local area give away things they no longer want. Not only do you give your rubbish a second life, you can pick up some useful things and meet like-minded people. Just go to www.freecycle.org for details of your local groups.

Repair don't replace

At one time every town would have at least one shop that repaired small appliances. Anything from a hair dryer to a vacuum cleaner could be taken in and most often picked up a few days later as good as new.

Sadly these repairers have gone. When you can buy a new hair dryer for as little as £10, how can it be economically repaired? So the broken appliance goes in the bin and a new one keeps the global economy turning, using up the planet's resources faster and faster. I'm convinced that in the future there will be an industry mining our waste tips for raw materials that we've discarded as having no value, and they'll wonder at our wastefulness.

You'd be surprised how many things can be repaired if you try, but do be careful with electrical equipment. There's an interesting charity in London (hopefully they'll expand) called The Restart Project who hold events where people take their broken electrical products and volunteers mend them and show visitors how to do it as well.

On their website, https://therestartproject.orgs, there's lots of helpful information and guidance on repairing things and, if it can't be repaired, how to dispose of it responsibly.

Skips and second-hand bargains

Skips are full of useful things others no longer want. I find it hard to pass one without taking a look. One man's scrap wood is another man's raised bedside, or just what is needed to repair a frame. At worst it's kindling for the woodburner.

Don't just dive into a skip without asking; the contents actually belong to the person who has dumped the items. It's not polite and technically theft. I've never been refused; in fact the request has often resulted in more prizes being brought out from the back.

The local paper is another good method of turning your unwanted goods into money and picking up second-hand bargains. Don't forget the charity and second-hand shops, either. You'll be amazed at what people donate. I'm writing this wearing a designer Yves St Laurent shirt purchased for just a pound from Help the Aged. (I think I was the aged being helped in this case, with a 95 per cent discount off the new price.) Our solid oak dining table would cost at least ten times what we paid for it in a second-hand shop, and less than we would have paid for a cheap and nasty new one from a national chain store.

Don't be afraid of or look down on second-hand; it's real recycling, making full use of our resources. It's true that you can't pick up exactly what you want when you want it, but that's half the fun. One word of warning, though: bargain hunting in second-hand shops is great fun but it can become very addictive!

CHAPTER TWENTY-ONE

Skills

It's all very well telling people to do things for themselves and save money, but often we pay others to do jobs for us because we lack the appropriate skills. So, the question is: how do we acquire these skills?

Nowadays we have a wonderful tool in the Internet. The sheer amount of information out there is mind-boggling. Never in the history of the human race has so much been made available to so many, and usually at very low cost. However, it's the volume of information that is the biggest barrier to finding what you are looking for.

The search engines, especially Google, are incredibly good at finding things but we need to help them to help us find exactly what we want. Just putting in a one-word search will usually result in masses of results, most not being what we want. For example, if I want to find out how to fix a dripping tap, then I might search for 'plumbing' – this gives me over 50 million results! 'Plumbing problems' drops this down to a mere half a million pages, but 'dripping tap' brings up 200,000 pages, and the first page even includes two videos showing how to sort it out.

The trick to finding what you want is to search carefully and to use phrases rather than just one word. I often use the Internet to figure out computer problems, and 99 per cent of the time putting in the obscure and incomprehensible error message I have received will provide the answer I want.

One strong word of warning: not everything you find on the Net is correct. It's worth checking two or, better still, three sources to confirm the accuracy of the information given.

Your next stop is a book. If you just want to fix a dripping tap the Net is great, but if you want to install a new central heating system a book is what you need. A book will go into more detail than the average web page, and the information is all to hand to refer to as and when you need it.

A book will give you a wider overview of a subject as well. Web pages tend to be very specifically targeted. If they're not, then the search engines don't deliver them to enquirers and nobody finds them anyway.

A great source for anybody researching is the local library. It's a tremendous shame how many have been closed in recent years as councils seek to save money. Not only do libraries have books to borrow on the shelves, they also have librarians. For me, the real resource is the librarian. He or she is trained in helping people find information and takes a real pride in finding the most appropriate and helpful works for you. If it's not on the shelves, then the librarian can usually obtain a copy for you – even out-of-print works don't seem to be a problem.

Not everything can be picked up from a book or video. For some things there is no substitute for a teacher. Local colleges, schools and universities run hundreds of courses in almost any subject you can think of. When people talk of night school, they often just think of flower-arranging courses but you will be surprised what you can find. I had the privilege of a twenty-week course in database design taught by a full-blown professor for the grand sum of £40 at a local university. That was just £1 an hour.

Short courses on practical subjects like plumbing, joinery and bricklaying could save you hundreds or thousands of pounds over the years; plus the satisfaction of doing a job yourself far outweighs whatever reward there may be in paying somebody else to do it. Your library will have the details.

Formal courses are not the only way to find teachers. If you want to keep poultry, it's well worth spending some time with another poultry keeper. Most of what's involved can be picked up from books, but advice from someone with real experience is invaluable.

I can't imagine learning how to handle bees from a book, and I've read some pretty good books on beekeeping. What they can't teach is the calmness of approach required to avoid provoking the bees. The reassurance of an experienced beekeeper just can't be duplicated in print.

Often there are local societies for most hobbies and, once again, your local library will help you find them. If you can't find a local society, seek out the national organisation who will know the nearest branch.

If you're having work done on your house, ask the workman if you can watch or even help. You can learn the skills needed for many simple jobs in this way. The more skills you have in your bag, the less you have to pay for in the future.

Some jobs you can't just pick up easily, for example gas fitting. There's a good reason for this. Although gas is no longer poisonous, an explosion or carbon monoxide poisoning can do more than just ruin your day. That's why it is illegal for unqualified people to touch gas appliances.

With electrical works you need to be careful – legal minefield warning! – but there is nothing to stop you working with a qualified electrician. In effect, you do the less-skilled work under his guidance and he signs off on it at the end.

If you find yourself needing to renovate a house or even just fit a new kitchen, then working with tradesmen will teach you a lot and reduce your costs – and it's surprising how few corners get cut when the boss is helping. You must make your intentions clear, though, or things can get acrimonious, which helps no one.

The term 'university of life' is very apt. You need to treat everything as an opportunity to acquire new skills and although you will be a Jack of all trades, master of none, Jack (or Jill) is all you need to be for many jobs.

CHAPTER TWENTY-TWO

Money

Money may be the root of all evil, but living without it is not easy – just try offering to pay your council tax with home-made chutney! I'm not able to give financial advice. For that you need to be qualified, just like those clever City chaps who told us endowments were the way to pay off a mortgage and private pension plans would ensure a wealthy early retirement. And yes, that is sarcasm.

I have learned a few lessons along the way, however, that you might find helpful. The first is just your attitude to money. Never forget how hard and long you have worked to earn it. You have exchanged your time for that money, and time on the earth is a scarce resource.

Many of us work for companies where the culture is to work long hours. The first to leave the office on time gets a black mark as if they were a skiver. Years ago I was an area manager with a large chain of shops to look after. One day I sat outside one of the shops waiting for it to open, talking with another area manager. We calculated the hours we worked and what we earned, and realised that we earned less per hour then the lowest-paid assistants. We just worked a lot more hours.

That was a sobering revelation; nobody lies on his deathbed wishing he'd spent more time on the shop floor. So, work out what your money has cost you in time and don't forget to base your calculations on your take-home pay after tax. This really changes your attitude to spending. No longer is something just a fiver, now it's half an hour's work. It can also be the prod you need to change your life and find a job where you may earn a little less cash but you work a lot less. This means you have time to save some money by doing for yourself what you would previously have bought with that cash.

Take control of your money

Don't forget that before you spend money, you've got to cover your basics. You've got your mortgage or rent, your fuel bills, insurance and all those other things that you have to pay for each month or year. It's well worth sitting down with the bank statements and making a list. Knowing what you have to spend enables you to see what you've really got left at the end of the month. That surplus money – technically it's called disposable income – is what you really can spend.

Don't overspend, whatever the excuse or reason.

Since some things are paid annually, open a savings account and put a bit away each month to cover them. Often you can pay things like a TV licence over time, but it's cheaper to pay in one go. It may not be sophisticated financial advice, but it does make life a lot simpler and easier.

When it comes to savings accounts, banks seem to have a nasty habit of initially offering good interest rates to attract savers and then quietly reducing them. That 'super saver bonus high interest account' ends up paying less than the 'everyday saver' – keep an eye on your rates.

If you've ever had the experience of walking into work to be given a redundancy notice (and I hope you never do), then having some savings will give you at least a breathing space to sort out another job. I try to keep enough money back to last for two months, but even a month's money is a huge help when you've suddenly no money coming in.

Credit cards are wonderful. Years back we told our five-year-old daughter that we didn't have any pennies to buy sweeties. She thought for a minute and said, 'Put it on Access!' There's no better way to get in a mess than credit cards; it's just so easy and convenient. With the growth of online shopping, cards are almost indispensable but you need to be firm with yourself. If you can't control your spending, cut them up. It's just too easy to get in a mess in a short time that can then take years to get sorted. When I took control of my money it took nearly two years to clear my credit-card debt. It's immensely satisfying to pay one off, cut up the card and close the account.

In Charles Dickens' novel *David Copperfield,* the character Wilkins Micawber states, 'Annual income twenty pounds, annual expenditure nineteen nineteen six, result happiness. Annual income twenty pounds, annual expenditure twenty pounds nought and six, result misery.' This was something that Dickens probably learned from his father John, who ended up in a debtors' prison.

We don't have debtors' prisons any more, thank goodness, but debt places an enormous strain onto us. It causes family break-up, stress and depression, and even results in suicide. Dickens' advice is as true today as it was 150 years ago.

If things have gotten out of control and beyond you, get proper independent advice. You need someone on your side. Those people who offer to help you get out of debt, to make arrangements with your creditors or whatever as advertised on the TV are *not* on your side. Their aim is to make more money out of you and your problem.

Citizens Advice should be your first call if you can't cope. They'll be able to give the best advice for your situation and point you to other sources of help. The library will have the contact details for the nearest branch to you, or visit their website, www.citizensadvice.org.uk. Another very useful port of call is the National Debtline, a charity that provides free impartial advice, at www.nationaldebtline.co.uk.

Being in debt enslaves you. It forces you to spend your precious time earning money to pay interest to banks, and they love it. It's far better to do without the latest gadgets and gizmos rather than suffer from debt. Low-cost living gives you freedom from that pressure. Doing without the latest games console or a new car means you have a happier life with more time for the things that really matter.

I've seen children with so many toys they don't know what to play with, yet they're deprived. I don't mean they're wanting for anything money can buy. They're deprived of the most precious gift you can give your children: your time and attention. A walk in the countryside each weekend means far more than a Playstation or even two days in Disneyland.

Work out what things are worth to you

Having got to grips with your money, what it costs you in terms of work to acquire and what you really have to spend, then you can decide what things are worth to you. Doing things for yourself takes time, so there is a cost; but you don't have enough time or the skills to do everything for yourself.

Often it takes longer to do something for yourself than to earn the money to buy something. But having said that, if you enjoy doing something then it isn't work; it's fun that makes a contribution.

Let me explain. I love growing my own vegetables. I get fresh air and exercise, and immense satisfaction in sitting down to a meal where everything on the plate has been grown by me. I know the hours spent growing those vegetables could be spent working to earn money to buy vegetables from the shops, and probably fewer hours as well. But – and it's a big but – I enjoy growing vegetables and don't particularly enjoy working!

My wife loves making jams, chutneys, butter and cheese. All those things save us money but they're not 'work'. They're fun that provides a financial bonus, not slavery.

You don't need money for everything you buy. Before we had money, we had barter. Now there is no way you can run a modern industrial society without money. Trust me, it's the only way our global village can function. However, barter can work well on an occasional individual basis.

I happen to be good with computers but not a very good plumber. I've been known to create impromptu indoor water features by changing a tap. So, I swapped a few hours setting up the plumber's new PC and he spent an hour replacing a tap for me. Nothing formal, nothing in writing, just a favour for a favour.

It's surprising how many skills you and your friends have between you. Swapping those skills or even goods you've made rather than formal cash is efficient so long as both parties feel they have had value.

Extra money and working from home

Few of us are fortunate enough that we wouldn't like some extra money, and a second job working from home can seem an ideal way to get it. There are some benefits to working from home, but drawbacks too that you need to consider. I work from home all the time and I love it, but it's not always ideal.

Usually there are no legal problems working from home so long as you're not having business visitors or customers to your house, but do be careful if you manufacture or hold stock at home. Your insurance company won't pay out if you burn the house down because your candle-making enterprise went wrong. Check on your insurance and with the mortgage company before leaping in.

Where to work can be a problem. I need a separate room to write in. There's no way I can concentrate, spread out research materials or find my scribbled notes if the family are around me or, worse still, the desk has been tidied. That's a job for a trained archaeologist! A friend has insulated his garden shed and that's now his corporate HQ. It's peaceful, snug and, most importantly, when he's in the shed the family know he's at work.

You need to have the family on your side when you work from home; they must understand that when you are working you are at work. I found that relatives and friends confused working from home with being unemployed and having time for their every call. Explain firmly that you're at work right now and you'll get back to them when you're finished. They'll learn pretty quickly.

The plus side of working from home is that there is no time wasted getting to work – for me it's three steps from the kitchen kettle to the office. You can pick your own hours of work, but do watch out as that can end up being every waking hour if you're not careful.

Something I didn't expect is that I do miss the companionship of having colleagues and workmates to talk to. Working from home can be a bit lonely.

So how do you earn this extra income from home? You can start your own business, turning a hobby into an income, or work for someone else. It's amazing how many hobbies can actually turn into a handy second income. If it's something you enjoy, then it's hardly work either.

The range of things you can do is limited only by your imagination. It is important that you enjoy whatever you do. If you don't it becomes a real chore, and there's a real difference between things made with love and those made with money in mind. You can't compete with mass production on their terms; your pride in the work is the real selling point.

Perhaps you make fabulous preserves, or you enjoy making or decorating cakes. I know people who run quite profitable sidelines selling their produce. With food products you need to consider hygiene and check out with the environmental health department of your local council.

Perhaps you enjoy woodwork. I know a chap who now makes fantastic bespoke furniture in his spare time. Each piece is individual, and you'd be hard-pressed to find that level of quality in a shop. He really didn't want to sell his work but when his house was full, his wife insisted.

You can make soap at home. I don't think you can save much money but it's interesting, and you can make individual fragranced soaps just as you want. There's no need to stop at soap, either. There's no reason why you can't make your own range of individual toiletries, bath salts, salves and scented oils. That's how the Body Shop started. We buy our soap from a lady who now has her own mini-factory in a garden shed, and very good it is too.

I know another lovely lady who sells embroidered towels and

aprons. She puts your name and a small design onto the towel. They make fantastic gifts and don't cost much so they're very popular, especially around Christmas. She enjoys it and makes a few pennies into the deal.

If you keep bees, then it's not just honey you can sell but other products made from your bees: beeswax candles for starters, or royal jelly. In business terms they call this 'added value'. The ingredients of jam may only cost 20 per cent of the price it sells for. The jam maker adds value in manufacturing.

The possibilities are endless and, if things work out, you may end up giving up your day job. The golden rule is not to expect much to start with and not to spend any money you wouldn't have done anyway on your hobby. That way you're not taking any risks and if the business does take off, it's all a bonus.

There comes a point with hobby work where you will need to consider tax and so forth. At that point you really need professional advice; a good accountant actually saves you money. And keeps you within the law!

Working for others is different. There are an awful lot of jobs advertised that are really not worth the phone call to apply for them. Stuffing envelopes or delivering leaflets are both mind-numbing and paid so badly they're a joke, albeit not a funny one. So check it out carefully. Ask yourself what they are really offering.

Then there are the 'business opportunities'. Most often they're opportunities to make money for someone else. One thing that always seems to raise its head when times are tough is 'multi-level marketing'. The idea is that you recruit others to sell some product and take a cut from their sales. They recruit others and take a cut, you take a cut and so on it goes. The problem is that the product itself, whatever it may be, has to be really expensive to accommodate all those cuts in price. In fact, the vast majority of stock sold in multi-level marketing schemes is sold to people who intend (notice that 'intend') to sell it on. Warning words to look for are 'downline' and 'upline'. If you hear those, run – and run fast.

Franchises are different. The theory is that someone else has developed a business that works and all you have to do is follow what they've done to make a successful business yourself. Many are genuine and, if it suits you, good business opportunities. Before jumping in, get professional advice. Consult a lawyer and an accountant. If it seems so good that you wonder why everyone isn't doing it, there is probably a catch somewhere. Check them out on the British Franchise Association website (www.thebfa.org) where there is a wealth of information.

The Internet has become a happy hunting ground for 'marketing gurus' who will show you how to make a fortune without doing any work. All you need to do is to send them some money for the secret details of their training course, which you need to make you wealthy overnight.

It's a classic sting, relying on greed. You're going to get something for nothing – well, nearly nothing. It's most often $97 and downloadable. Of course it's a con: they make their money from you. If their scheme was so good, then they wouldn't be selling it to you. A little more subtle than those gentlemen from Nigeria who email to ask for your help in extracting $10 million from some bank. Yet people keep falling for it.

The Internet does offer more possibilities for working from home than we've ever had before. There are people making a living from buying and selling on auction sites like eBay, but a word of warning. If things go wrong, do not expect any real help from the auction site provider. My experience is that you get automated irrelevant replies, often pointing you to web pages that don't help you anyway, and if you do get through to a human being there's not much help there either.

The one rule on any business investment you must keep in mind is that it is a bet. No matter how good the odds appear, there is always the chance it will go horribly wrong and you'll lose your money. So never risk more than you can afford to lose.

Finally, keep in mind that true wealth is happiness. Money is useful, but happiness is priceless. Spend less and be happy.

Useful Websites

www.allotment-garden.org

www.lowcostliving.co.uk

www.chickens.allotment-garden.org

www.britishbee.org.uk

www.hetas.co.uk

www.energysavingtrust.org.uk

www.cyclescheme.co.uk

www.freecycle.org

https://therestartproject.org

www.citizensadvice.org.uk

www.nationaldebtline.co.uk

www.thebfa.org

Index